THE HOSTAGE

A Drama : By PAUL CLAUDEL

*Translated from the French, with an
Introduction by* PIERRE CHAVANNES

New Haven: YALE UNIVERSITY PRESS
London: HUMPHREY MILFORD :: OXFORD
UNIVERSITY PRESS ✌ MDCCCCXVII

CONTENTS

	PAGE
Introduction	1
Persons of the Play	21
Act One : Scene One	23
Act One : Scene Two	53
Act Two : Scene One	76
Act Two : Scene Two	98
Act Three : Scene One	117
Act Three : Scene Two	125
Act Three : Scene Three	142
Act Three : Scene Four	145
Act Three : Scene Five	152
Acting Version Substituted for Scenes Four and Five of the Original Text	161

Introduction

The Yale University Press does itself honour in publishing this book, the second drama of Paul Claudel to appear in English. "The Hostage" bears little resemblance to those theatrical works which sooner or later cross the Atlantic as a matter of course, even when they are not definitely written with a view to exportation. Like the other plays of Claudel, "The Hostage" has nothing in common with that facile art whose sole aim is to fill up—or while away—an evening for us with amusing adventures at once forgotten; with that art which is most at home in the region of the commonplace, timidly shunning the heights where dizziness threatens, and the depths where there is risk of losing one's footing in unaccustomed gloom. "The Hostage" is fundamentally opposed to that type of play in which virtuosity and "métier" count for more than soul and true art, in which interest is derived from the cleverness of the intrigue and from the complication of the action, a wholly material type, in which content counts for less than externals, intellectual beauty for less than volatile emotion, author less than actor, actor less than costume and scenery; tending, in a word, towards a kind of cinema, seeking in vain to hide the poverty of the thought by the lavishness of the concrete expression. "The Hostage" is the work of a great poet; it speaks to the noblest in us and can therefore only leave us nobler. Rooted firmly in the past, fed by vigorous thought, written in a language of incomparable richness, the material element counts for nothing in this drama, soul and true art count for everything.

* * * * * * * *

Differing in this from the other plays of Claudel, which are either set in a visionary Middle Age, or seem to unfold outside of time, "The Hostage" is closely bound up with historical events. The action takes place at a definite moment; and this moment is a pre-eminently tragic one. Napoleon with his immense armies has plunged into the depths of Russia, and over the world emptied of that mighty presence a deep silence hangs, a stupor weighs. The "Emperor of the French" is still the all-powerful emperor of the continent; and yet, in this silence, there is an uneasiness and a strange expectancy. If an adventurer, by a bold stroke, could master Paris and the great machine of government for a time, men might well ask whether the Colossus was as powerful as he seemed. The Legitimist party still has faithful adherents, and its agents are active in the shadows. The arm of the balance hesitates for a moment at the height of its course, and we feel that it is about to begin its descent. Such is the state of affairs when, on a stormy night, the door of Coûfontaine Abbey opens; and Sygne, sitting over her day's accounts, sees her cousin, Viscount George de Coûfontaine et Dormant, Lord Lieutenant of the King for Lorraine and Picardy, enter the room.

George is one of those soldiers of the King who, although he is unable to defend the Royalist cause by the sword, defends it by intrigue, by conspiracy, in case of necessity, by crime: interviews and secret missions of the King in England, nightly disembarkings on some unfrequented shore in Brittany, disguises, tricks to deceive the imperial police, enterprises a hundred times baffled and a hundred times attempted, cryptic messages, nights spent in the woods and days in small and obscure hiding places—such is his life. Sygne, in the meantime, has been secretly engaged in a long struggle of another sort. Patiently, silently, she is joining together bit by bit the land of the Coûfontaines which has been cut up by the Revolution, in order to restore whole the heritage of her ancestors to the head of her house, to the male line of her race, to her cousin George and to his children. This monastic house in which she lives—all that remains of the old château which was demolished and burnt down— is one of George's places of refuge in his adventurous and tragic life. On this night, he does not arrive alone. He brings with him an old priest riding on an ass, a precious capture which he confides to this safe place for a few days.

Although these historic events come within the scope of the play, they remain in the background; only the distant rumour of them reaches us. Claudel has avoided that superficial and undistinguished method of dramatizing history which relies for its effects on quotations from documents, tags of historic phrases and touches of local colour, introducing so-called "real" personages, and depending largely on what is conventionally regarded as "picturesque"—in a word, the whole paraphernalia of historical veneer. Rigorous exactitude in detail matters little to him; the very adventure which is the basis of the play is imagined, and everything turns—except the last scene, which is not an integral and necessary part of the play—around four persons, five at most.

In this drama the conflict is one of ideas—ideas which are not sheer abstractions, but vital forces contending for mastery and serving as the substructure of the events which they determine. The conflict lies in the opposition between the idea of the old order of things and the idea of the Revolution.

George and Sygne de Coûfontaine may indeed remind us of the passionate loyalty of a George Cadoudal, or of some of the defenders and martyrs of the Legitimist faith at the time of the Empire; but they are something more than these. With that nobleness, and that purity of nobleness, with that lofty and sad consciousness of their destiny and of their duties, which often mark the last representatives of a doomed race, George and Sygne represent and incarnate the old monarchical and feudal order which the centuries of history and of faith had slowly built up. It was an order which was based on inequality, yet in which there were really neither privileged nor exploited classes, because jealousy, the fruit of the struggle for equality, did not exist, all sharing the life of all, "the poor man enjoying the riches of the rich, the monk the pleasure of the worldling, the worldling the prayers of the monk, and for all there was art, poetry, religion." It was an order in which the relations between men were not governed by contracts but were based on traditional loyalty: the submission and fidelity of a man to his lord, of a vassal to his liege, and the protection of the chieftain whose part was to "serve in commanding"; an order in which man finds his chieftain at birth, in which all had the king, their chieftain and father, above them, in whose family all families were represented and united; an order so old that it seemed founded, not on the caprice of men, but on the very nature of things— eternal.

With horror and despair, with a religious anger and the revolt of their whole being, George and Sygne see arising the new society in which old bonds are broken, old duties abolished, former reverence and former respect despised; in which there remains nothing but an anarchic mob of impotent individuals; in which man, in order to obey man no more, has bowed to an impersonal machine, an anonymous idol, the stupid will of the majority; in which, in the place of traditional loyalties, there is no longer anything to hold men together but the shifting combinations of interest. Thus George exclaims:

"I look around me and there is no longer any society among men,

But only the 'law,' as it is called, and the machine-printed text, an inanimate will, a stupid idol.

Where there are rights there is no longer affection.

. . . Can a society continue in which every man believes it exists at the expense of his own rights? Nay, force cannot replace sacrifice . . ."

These ideas undoubtedly contradict some of the dearest and most universal beliefs and prejudices of our time. Yet while we may discuss without accepting them, we cannot reject them disdainfully. They obsessed all the thinkers of the nineteenth century who had a passion for the dignity of man and who felt the burden of the great interests of human conscience. Some have accepted them in despair; others, equally unsatisfied with the present, have escaped the grip of the past by projecting their dreams into the future. But every noble conscience has been troubled by them. Under each word of the discussions of Sygne and Turelure, of the conversations between Sygne and George, a scholiast of the future might insert by way of footnote a page of J. de Maistre, Burke, Bonald, Balzac, A. Comte, Le Play, Taine, or (to name a more recent writer) of Maurras, as this extract from Renan might be inserted:

"Suppress this great law (that the human task is indivisible and demands for its accomplishment inequalities which are not an injustice), put all individuals on the same grade with equal rights, without the bond of submission to a common task, and you have mediocrity, isolation, barrenness, the impossibility of living, something like the life of our time, the saddest, even for the common people, that has been lived . . .

"The Revolution was definitively irreligious and atheistic. The society which it imagined, in the sad days which followed the onset of fever, when it sought to collect itself, is a sort of regiment made up of materialists, in which discipline takes the place of virtue. The wholly negative basis which the dry and hard men of that time gave to French society can only produce a roguish and ill-mannered people; their code, a work of defiance, admits as its first principle that everything is reckoned in money, that is to say, in pleasure. Jealousy summarises all the moral theory of these would-be founders of our laws. Now jealousy is the foundation of equality, not liberty; always putting man on his guard against the encroachments of his fellow creatures, it prevents affability between different classes. There is no society without affection, without tradition, without respect, without mutual amenity . . ."

The conflict continues in every man who thinks. Claudel, who has in his blood something of Coûfontaine and also of Turelure, of noble and commoner, has felt it with especial violence. Tête d'Or, the hero of his first drama, expresses this aristocratic revolt of the individual against the crowd, of the proud, strong, untamed person against weak cowardice. Sygne is a feminine Tête d'Or who, instead of seeking her law in herself like an anarchist, accepts it, ready made, from without, with her traditional order of things. And who has not in him, in one way or another, something of Coûfontaine and Turelure, and of their struggle?

* * * * * * * *

George and Sygne are soldiers of a defeated cause.

"Many other things, more beautiful still, come to an end with us," cries George. He struggles bravely, but without hope:

"Cut off, despoiled, inflexible, fruitless . . .

Those things alone which are dead, vanquished and impossible are mine."

And, moreover, all the efforts of Sygne prove to be in vain: the land which her patient sacrifice has pieced together, the land that is bound to the past and to the life of the Coûfontaines with an indissoluble bond, will never belong to George's children, but will go to Turelure's child, of which she herself will be the mother, Sygne the proud soul, the untamed aristocrat. Here is the tragedy of those large domains that are rich with the past, whose façades of grey stone used to ennoble the countryside of France, and whose foliage above the park wall threw its beautiful shadows on all the windings of the "Chaussée du Roy"; the park has been divided, the trees cut down, often the château has been destroyed, or has been overtaken by a still sadder fate—the steward has installed himself in the master's house; the lawyer who lay in wait for his prey in the depths of his chambers, or the business man from the town, has purchased it at the sale of the "biens nationaux." The feudal idea is dead—and it died of itself, of internal disorders, before succumbing to external onslaughts—George and Sygne are alone in a new world:

"Have men still need of us with them?" asks Sygne. "No more than of Coucy and its towers."

And Sygne will be conquered, taken by force by her servant's son, and carried a prisoner into the hostile camp:

"And so now I stand alone in an enemy's land,
Like that Agénor of olden time whose castle stood on the other side of the Dead Sea, on the banks of Arnon."

"Let Coûfontaine perish," cried George, "so long as

the King is restored with France." The King is restored, but by Turelure; a constitutional king, bound by a charter, a superior prefect, only a "Turelure crowned." Royalty is dead.

In this great disaster of their life and faith it seems as if everything were gone; in this present, in which their past meets its death, it seems as if there were no more room for anything solid, or enduring, anything which remains when the individual is gone or when his caprice alters, anything royal because eternal. But if everything is over for George, the King's servant, not everything is over for Sygne, the King's servant, but also the servant of God, and of the Church whose cause she identifies with that of God. The old man whom George brings to her,—"poor foolish George"—this old man whom she is to save at the price of the most terrible sacrifice, is the Pope, the frail old prisoner who makes his appearance only to disappear again immediately from this drama which he determines without knowing it. The Pope with his few "black cardinals"[1] can alone cope with Napoleon, he who opposes all powers and for whose possession all powers contend, the hostage, seized by Napoleon in irritation at this independence, the hostage snatched from the Emperor by George to strengthen the Royalist cause, the hostage seized by Turelure to serve his ambition, who

---

[1] This name was given to the cardinals who supported the Pope in his fight for spiritual domination. Napoleon gave orders, in a measure, that thenceforth they should wear black stockings; a few were exiled to the country or imprisoned at Vincennes. Those cardinals who became the Emperor's tools still wore red stockings.

9

is in the power of all, yet belongs to none of them.[2]
Sygne has saved the papacy, which is the "inheritor of
all kingdoms, all destinies and all paternities"—

"The King is dead, the Chief is dead. But I have
saved the eternal Priest.

God is living with us, so long as we have His word
yet with us, and a little bread, and His sacred Hand
which binds and unbinds."

Here again, even if we do not share his faith, we
must recognise the greatness that it gives to Claudel's
thought. There is in Claudel a natural genius that is
robust and even somewhat heavy, complex and strongly
sensuous; but there is also in him a logician enamoured
of vast systems of thought, a theologian who has worked
out finally his disciplines and his forms. He is, we might
say, a romantic who has laid upon himself a classic
discipline; and by this constant reaction of his "rational
soul" on his "sensory soul" Claudel is indeed a Latin
and a Roman. We may disagree as to the effects of his
conversion and his long struggle on his art. But in this
will to find a base that is fixed, certain, eternal in the
moral world, in this will to build upon a foundation of
rock—to build with the genuine craftsmanship of the
cathedrals, and according to their marvellously geomet-
rical plans, a stone edifice above the surge which ebbs
and flows—there is a certain attraction and grandeur.

[2] At the time of the Russian campaign Pope Pius VII was Napoleon's
prisoner at Fontainebleau—the dramatic turns of that struggle between
Pope and Emperor are well known. He was only set free by the defeat
of Napoleon in March, 1814.

This solidity, this passion for solidity, we feel in the very plan of the play, in the construction of this drama "in three acts, each consisting of scenes which have in turn a simple and severe design; a plan as formal as that of the three porches of the Gothic cathedral, each divided from the other by a stone mullion."

* * * * * * * *

But to insist thus, at the outset, on the idea, and even on the conflict of the ideas of the drama, is to run the risk of falsifying its significance. "The Hostage" is not a social pamphlet or a problem play, the characters are not resonant and well-worn speaking-trumpets for the author's ideas. They live their own lives. And yet, we must confess, the genius of Claudel is lyric rather than dramatic. In his early dramas his heroes often seem mere symbols, or characters in outline, or diverse voices answering and opposing one another in the poet's soul, rather than living heroes. Lyricism in "The Hostage," instead of being developed for itself, is more bound up with the action; the action springs not only from the shock of ideas and sentiments of the dramatist, but these ideas and sentiments are incarnate in characters who are varied types, each with a personal life that is unforgettable. No doubt all these characters speak the language of Claudel, an eloquent and familiar language, rich with thought and feeling, and yet Turelure does not speak like George or George even like Sygne. Each has his own lyric accent, one might say his own inner music; each has his voice which we hear. Few scenes at the theatre attain to the dramatic intensity of the first scene of this play, the purity and nobility of which remind us of Sophocles; or even to that of the entire second act with its duel between Sygne and Turelure, a duel that is concealed at the outset under the mask of good fellowship, though it is artfully hinted at, and then suddenly is fought out with a brutality that hurts; and to that of the other struggle immediately afterwards between Sygne and Badilon, between Sygne and herself, her revolts and lacerations, until she accepts the supreme sacrifice. There is a struggle not only of ideas, or even of wills, as in Corneille, but of men and women of flesh and blood and of passion.

"Ah! I am deaf and do not hear," Sygne protests to Badilon, "and I am a woman and not a nun, made wholly of wax and manna like an *Agnus Dei!*"

We hear the voice of Sygne, "clear and melodious that has in it at times a note of strange sweetness, almost painful," or that of George, always "even, measured and rather low." We think we hear also the voice of Turelure and the voice of Father Badilon. But in these voices there is an accent that comes from some source more remote than they. These people have in their blood other passions, other desires, other aversions than their own; the generations before are continued and live and speak in them. Sygne and George, it is true, share that spirit of heroism, that high conception of honour and that passion of loyalty which inspire the warriors of the *chansons de geste,* as well as the argumentative, strong-willed and generous heroes of Corneille. But they are also more nearly related to the soil of France, and they know it.   They are conscious, not only of their existence, but of their roots—and when the tree is torn up do we not then learn of its roots?   Turelure himself, Baron Toussaint Turelure, that plebeian Talleyrand, jeering, uncouth, cunning, so much at his ease in his day, remains the son of the gamekeeper's daughter and Quiriace the Wizard, who once poached in the château woods.   To what depths of a bygone peasantry, of submission and revolt, he goes back, with his deep covetousness of the soil, his disdain of old conventions, and at the same time that instinct which makes him ally himself with the race of his former masters—in order to conquer and humiliate it, but also in his eager desire, perhaps not altogether vile, to turn to Sygne "his face full of crimes and despair."   And it is the same with Badilon, "the poor little urchin," who, thanks to the Countess Renée, became a priest, who remains of the village, who belongs to the château, and who is essentially of the Church; the clumsy rustic, "the good fellow whom a bottle of wine on occasion does not frighten," "the imbecile, the coarse man heavy with flesh and sins," but also the priest; for the rough red hand which lifted the glass is that same hand which . . . "has so often given you the sacrament and elevates, each morning, The Son of God in the elements."

The rustic in him remains full of a hereditary respect for the daughter of his lords, full of admiration for the nobility of her soul; but when the rustic turns priest he speaks with an admirable and odious mixture of authority, of superiority, and at the same time of inhumanity, with that peculiar conception of truth and honour that we can only describe as ecclesiastic. To Sygne, who pleads to him the sacred oath by which she has confirmed her pledge to her cousin—an oath which it is, however, in the interest of the Church to break—"an oath in the night,"—Badilon replies that it was a matter of "promises only and neither deed nor sacrament."

There is also a certain dualism in Claudel's literary style. But no translation can preserve the richness—and justness—of this language, any more than it can preserve its beautiful wavelike rhythm.

* * * * * * * *

A conflict of ideas, of opposing faiths, of human beings, "The Hostage" is also, and primarily, a conflict of conscience. There is in it, from the outset, a silent presence which reveals itself in obscure hints—like the threat of fatality in ancient drama; to George who says to her, "You are abiding and true," Sygne replies: "God alone is true," and later on she also tells him: "God alone is infallible." There is "on the whitewashed wall a large wooden cross with a large crucifix, wild and mutilated in appearance." The wood of which the cross is made comes from two beams that survived the burning of the old house; the mutilated figure of Christ has been put together by Sygne from the pieces that were scattered far and wide. George, looking at the cross, cries:

"So, returning home, all that I find left of the house,

The beam and joist in form of a cross, and even that Thou hast taken for thyself, O Workman's Son, and there is no room for another."

"There is no room for another!" It is not until later that George is to understand all the significance, all the terrible gravity of these words. Sygne, when she, too, understands, turns towards the bronze crucifix and cries out in her agony:

"Woe is me because Thou hast visited me!"

The conflict in "The Hostage" is, at bottom, between Sygne and her God. In the end a horrible sacrifice is asked of her: her life, hitherto, has been merely one long sacrifice made to realise her dream; the dream goes, her life loses its *raison d'être*. And so with all her ardour, all her loyalty, all her nobleness, she has thrown herself towards the only one who remains to her, alone and despoiled like herself—and he also, on his part, has no other resource outside himself than in her alone. And lo, the priest demands that she shall break her promise, renounce her pledge, withdraw the hand she has placed in that of her cousin, unclasp by a deed of dishonour those hands which were conjoined in the past when in the sight of the children their parents were sent to the scaffold together, unclasp those hands conjoined, after that sacrament of blood, by the sacrament of honour, make a lie of the *"foi,"* the two clasped hands of the Coûfontaine coat of arms!

All this Badilon asks of her. To be sure, he does not demand it, and when Sygne's resistance weakens he seems terrified by the horror of the sacrifice to which he has driven her, and he speaks as though he wished to hold her back. But to propose a sacrifice in the way he does is to constrain some souls: the more heavy and cruel the sacrifice the more they think they cannot flinch from it without shame. Badilon tempts Sygne "according to her weakness," he tempts her according to her strength, until Sygne gives way overcome:

"Lord, Thy will be done and not mine!"

This is, in truth, the centre of the drama, and it is worth our while to stop a moment. Claudel has made the remark, *à propos* of "The Hostage" and the welcome given to it by the public, that the art of to-day, like the morals of to-day—which are timid renunciations, "Buddhisms on a small scale for the use of men of the world"—leaves to us unused much of our energy, and perhaps even the deepest and best part of man. It is unfortunate that moderns have forgotten the great school of energy, the mighty faith which determines that we are what we are, and not Hindoos or Chinese. "The demands of Christianity, apparently excessive and unreasonable, are the only ones, after all, which are really proportionate to our strength and our reason. They mutilate nothing, they are catholic, that is to say, universal; they appeal to the whole man, his intelligence, his will and his feelings; they compel us to be in a permanent state of mobilisation against passion, against easy doubts, and, for this perpetual war, we are not over-endowed with all our faculties . . ."[1] The demands of Christianity

[1] Extract from a letter of P. Claudel to "le Temps," June 28, 1914. This letter was written immediately after the production of "The Hostage." The drama was first acted by M. Lugne-Poe at the Œuvre Theatre, and then transferred to the Odéon, where it was performed with great success.

"mutilate nothing," as Claudel well says: they appeal to all powers in man, they do not claim to destroy them; they harmoniously increase their strength and delicacy by this continual struggle and constant exercise. But is it indeed this truth that we see in "The Hostage"? The sacrifice which Father Badilon asks of Sygne is not merely the sacrifice of her personal pride and of her pride as a noble. It is more and worse than this: it is, by the breaking of the pledged word that it involves, by the defilement that it imposes on that pure soul, a sacrifice of the highest, a sort of rape, a form of suicide. The sacrifice the cross demands of us is to transform, to lift our natures to a higher plane, not to destroy.

Can we say that it is really grace which has raised Sygne for an instant in order to let her fall again immediately to her noble maidenly pride and her natural violence? In that exaltation which carries her away there enter all those elements of her nature on which Badilon knew how to play in turn. He appeals to her noble and womanly generosity by evoking the feeble and despoiled Christ, who can do nothing without us; he appeals to her imagination and her pride by evoking the immense cloud of witnesses who surround her, "the blessed spirits in heaven, the sinners beneath our feet—and the human crowds, one on another, awaiting your resolution." "It was the bad blood in me which spoke," cries Sygne when George asks her why she made the sacrifice. It is not grace which has triumphed over natural pride, it is this pride, or rather this nobility of soul, this thrilling sense of honour which has turned back upon itself in order to be sacrificed:

"Great and unheard of things, our heart is such that it cannot withstand them."

"All our faculties," says Claudel again, "dwell in us unknown, and amid our vain bustle we have the sensation of nothingness which accompanies idleness if we do not embrace this cross, which exerts the highest tension on our whole being." ("De même toutes nos facultés nous demeurent comme inconnues, et parmi tous nos vains tracas nous avons cette sensation de néant qui accompagne l'oisiveté, si nous n'embrassons cette croix qui nous tend de toutes parts jusqu'à l'extrême."

Yet the life of Sygne is broken, the secret springs of her life are dried up, her service is over and her sacrifice does not give her entrance to a higher life. She yields her passions, her name, her body; she yields everything. But all this is no more than a corpse, and what of life remains in her is no more than a protest. Her head, with its mechanical movement, says No! The feeling of her shame is bound to her; she will hasten towards death because it is too good a thing to leave to others. To the priest's supreme appeal: "Sygne, soldier of Christ, arise!", to her ancestor's appeal: "Coûfontaine, adsum!", she shakes her head as if to say No; "all is finished."[1]

---

[1] It is only just to add that Claudel has himself felt this objection: in a new version of the last scene but one (the last scene of the play as presented on the stage), which will be found at the end of this translation, he has altered to a certain extent the form and the meaning of

INTRODUCTION

Just as the miracles of Christ in the Gospels are only
performed in defiance of death, and on behalf of life, so
the sacrifices He demands are in the interests of a higher,
a more complete life. In his enthusiasm Claudel goes
further than the Gospels. A Christian by a sudden
conversion after a long struggle with himself, Claudel
is one of those violent persons who take the Kingdom as
by storm. Is there not in "The Hostage" something of
that violence which has not yet achieved the harmony
and the peace of certainty, and which with savage and
desperate force shakes the cross that it embraces?

*   *   *   *   *   *   *   *

Like Badilon, Sygne may be mistaken, but she believes
herself called by her conscience and by the voice of her
God to the horrible sacrifice, and she obeys; the drama
is a drama of conscience. Perhaps even such reservations
as these we have made come from our modern sentimen-
tality, which recoils before the supreme demands of conscience, and which is terrified by the absolute in faith, in
submission, in sacrifice. In "The Hostage" there is

that moving scene in which Sygne dies, defeated, refusing to forgive.
It is Turelure and no longer Badilon whom the author—by an inspiration
in which buffoonery mingles with tragedy—imagines as summoning
Sygne to be loyal to her faith and to her God; and in vain, until the
moment when, bending over the dying woman, he cries aloud to her the
old Coûfontaine motto: "Coûfontaine, adsum!" This last appeal which
comes to her from the masters of her race and from the long line
of her dead ancestors, even though it is spoken by lips she hates, Sygne
cannot resist: like the dying soldier who stands erect once more on the
battle field when the flag goes past, she responds to the watchword of
the Coûfontaines: she raises herself erect, then falls back again, dead.

19

nothing of that art which Claudel described as "art that is soft, painted, art that goes nowhere, art in which nothing is orderly, art deprived of all sense as of all virtue." Claudel's art tends to the opposite extreme. The air into which he leads us is rare—is it that of the summit, or is it that of the desert?—it is rare and noble. Above this drama two trees stand erect, two kinds of wood: one is the Tree-Dormant, the great Coûfontaine oak which rose in the château court; the other is the wood of the cross made out of the two beams snatched from the fire. The seignorial tree has been uprooted, the Revolution has passed and left nothing of it—

"But this wood of which the cross is made will never fail."

PIERRE CHAVANNES.

THE HOSTAGE

A DRAMA

———

PAUL CLAUDEL

———

PERSONS OF THE PLAY

Pope Pius

Father Badilon

The King of France

Viscount Ulysses Agénor George de Coûfontaine et Dormant

Baron, then Count, Toussaint Turelure, Prefect of Marne, then of Seine

Sygne de Coûfontaine

And Others

Act One: Scene One

The Cistercian abbey of Coûfontaine, owned by
SYGNE. The library on the first floor: a large, lofty
room, lighted by four undraped windows with small,
greenish panes. At the back, between two high
doors, on the whitewashed wall, a large wooden cross
with a rude, bronze crucifix, which shows signs of
mutilation. At the other end, above SYGNE'S head,
on the remnant of a cool-coloured silk tapestry, in
which is an ornament of entwined foliage in the
middle of a tattered pastoral scene, is woven the
Coûfontaine coat of arms: or on a chief gules (two
clasped hands), azure on the point with a sword of
argent on a pale between Sun and Moon, and for
battle cry and motto: Coûfontaine, adsum!
   The floor, which is extremely clean, is of wide
plank studded with irregular rows of large shining
nails. SYGNE is sitting in a corner at a charming
little cabinet completely covered with account books
and neatly arranged bundles of papers. Farther
back is a small table on which are bread and wine
and other things. Large, formal pieces of furniture,
chairs and arm-chairs stand in a line down the whole
length of the room, which has an austere and de-

23

*serted appearance. A screen on which prunes are
drying stands on the floor.*

This is not all visible when the curtain goes up.

*It is night; the inside shutters are closed. The
room is lighted only by the wax taper on the table.*

Storm outside.

*A door opens, although no one is seen, and the
whistling of the wind is heard. The flame of the
candle flickers.* SYGNE *shields it with her hand.*

SYGNE (*looking toward the back of the room*):
    George!

COÛFONTAINE: Good evening, Sygne! Good morn-
    ing, rather.

        (*She clasps her hand to her heart as if
    overcome by emotion.* GEORGE *is seen in
    the half-lighted part of the room, a man
    of athletic build, who holds himself very
    erect.*

SYGNE:[1] Your room is ready.

COÛFONTAINE:[2] Presently.

I have no time for sleep. I have much to talk
    over with you.

It is a very long time since we saw each other,
    cousin.

                    (*She sits down again.*

---

[1] She speaks in a clear and melodious voice, that has in it at times
a note of strange sweetness, almost painful.

[2] He speaks without haste, always in an even, measured and rather
low tone.

SYGNE: I was ready for your arrival. All my accounts are here, clear and correct!

Never have I gone to bed without writing up my books for the day before saying my prayers.

Those there are for the police, and this small one is for you. By day as by night

Someone may come! You will find everything plain and in order.

COÛFONTAINE: The accounts! These accounts! That is always your first cry!

I see you are still the same, Sygne! Old Suzanne had in you a good pupil.

No one can teach writing like a master who cannot read.

But you have no accounts to render to me. Everything is yours.

SYGNE: Nay, it is yours, Monsieur.

You are the chief, and I the poor sibyl who keeps the fire burning.

COÛFONTAINE: I do not like this light.

SYGNE: The shutters are closed, inside and outside. Nothing can be seen. Even I can scarcely distinguish you.

COÛFONTAINE (*in a lower tone, raising his finger*): Is HE here?

SYGNE (*in the same tone*): He came two hours ago. Justin led him through the woods on the donkey.

25

COÛFONTAINE: What has he been doing?

SYGNE: He sat down, his hands on his knees, breathing heavily like a man about to pass away.

He asked for a priest, that he might make confession.

I sent for Father Badilon.

> (*Movement by* COÛFONTAINE.

You are vexed?

COÛFONTAINE: Go on.

SYGNE: I could not refuse him. He begged me so graciously, looking at me with his great dark eyes,

Speaking of his heart, in the manner of a priest, "the weight that is on his heart." What weight?

He confessed, and said mass immediately. I was present.

Ah, he was no longer the same man at the altar! No longer that thin shadow of a man! But an angel of great vehemence and gentleness, performing an act which is inestimable, the pontiff speaking in letters of gold!

Who is he, George?

COÛFONTAINE: He is resting?

SYGNE: He is resting. The priest has remained near him; he will say mass here.

> (*Gusts of wind outside.*

COÛFONTAINE: It was time we got under shelter.

I recognise my own native wind.

SYGNE: What a pity! The orchards were so fine! There will not be an apple left on the tree.

COÛFONTAINE: The storm is our protection. I am in great danger, Sygne!
I have dared to do an unheard of thing.

SYGNE: Whatever the peril, you are safe here with me!

COÛFONTAINE: I have never felt uneasy here.
That is why I have brought you my capture,
For which I am indebted to those poor eyes of our brother Toussaint,
With whom you are on good terms, I believe.

SYGNE: Cousin, I am a man of business, and may not choose my terms.

COÛFONTAINE: You must wed him. His arms, smeared on to ours,
Would enliven this old daub.

(He points to the tapestry.

SYGNE: Do not scoff.

COÛFONTAINE: I am jesting, Sygne. Shame on me! Now there are tears in your eyes!
You are so good, I cannot help it, I have to hurt you! It is my way of loving you.
Ah, what a youth is yours, my poor cousin!
Buying back and putting together again, bit by bit, this old estate,
Vineyards and fields, woods, sandy wastes and cultivated acres,

Like a piece of old torn lace that is caught together
thread by thread.

SYGNE: It is your property, Coûfontaine, that
Suzanne and I have gathered together.

COÛFONTAINE: Well fashioned, weaver!

Our mothers, with idle fingers, loved to unravel,

Ripping apart galoons and embroideries, undoing
the threads, one by one.

What they undid, you are gathering together
again.

My own cousin Sygne, who is more to me than
much gold and silver!

Why do they say of the lilies that they spin not?

Ah, cousin, if each of your fair brothers of France,

And all the daughters of noble houses, had done
as well, the King would be able to return,

There would be no rent in the old flag!

Alas, how many stitches are dropped when a
thread breaks!

SYGNE (*taking in her hands a miniature lying on the
table and gazing at it*): There they are! These
are my two loved ones, for whom it is well
worth while that I should take a little trouble.

Your children, George,—mine, too, may I not call
them? The fairy aunt, the fairy spider who
stayed behind in France must rebuild their
house for them there by her magic art.

For we who are caught between memory and duty
do not work for ourselves.

When shall I see them, George?   Adorable children!

The knight with his little whip already resembles
you, Coûfontaine, with his Picardian manner
and that air of command and importance.

And the little girl, how dear she is!

Their mother was complaining about them in her
last letter.   How could she have the heart?

COÛFONTAINE: That letter was written a long time
ago.

They are good now, and give her no trouble.

SYGNE: And how handsome their mother is, holding them in her beautiful arms!

O George, how eager you will be, when you return
from the war, to kiss this beautiful fresh rose,
in which shine six beautiful eyes.

I can well see what it was in her that pleased you,
it was that half-yielding, frankly arrogant air,
the full lip and low brow.

We work together, and I look at them sometimes,
glad at heart.

How beautiful are her eyes, like some fond young
creature who is giving her heart, and is eager to
know if you love her!

You are brave to leave her, Coûfontaine,—always
to rove far away!

COÛFONTAINE: We are both in the service of the King.

SYGNE: Does he always listen to you?

COÛFONTAINE: I fear I have lost something of my hold.

SYGNE: You have not offended him?

COÛFONTAINE: It was not in my power to keep my wife alive forever.

(*Silence.*

SYGNE: George, I do not understand! What horrible, poisoned words are you speaking?

COÛFONTAINE: Do you not know that my wife was the Dauphin's mistress?

Everybody envied my good fortune. I alone, fool that I was, knew nothing.

Death has revealed all.

SYGNE: She is dead then, George?

COÛFONTAINE: Give me that portrait.

SYGNE (*taking it quickly*): Do her no more harm! Dear one, here next my heart, you are safe.

COÛFONTAINE: It is the only likeness of them I have left.

(*She looks at him as if she does not understand.*

All that you hold in your hands is no more.

SYGNE: George!

COÛFONTAINE: You do not understand me? The two children . . .

30

SYGNE: Enough! Do not speak. Oh, not that! Not anything so horrible!

COÛFONTAINE: . . . are dead. Both died almost at the same time, while I was in France, of that virulent English fever.

SYGNE: God have pity on us!

> (SYGNE *stands quite still for a moment, her eyes closed, as if she were faint; then slowly she shakes her head like a person saying No.*

I suppose there is nothing I can say to you, George?

COÛFONTAINE: There is nothing to say.

> (*Pause.*

SYGNE: Come and get this paper which is here on the table.

> (*He approaches the table, and as he holds out his hand* SYGNE *seizes it in hers and bursts into tears, her face against his hand.* COÛFONTAINE *strokes her head in silence.*

COÛFONTAINE: You must not cry, Sygneau. Our name is now at an end, and we two alone are left.

So too many other things more beautiful still come to an end with us.

Everyone is not made to be happy.

Another pleased her and I could do nothing. I thought I loved her as much as it is possible to love.

And as for the children, a soldier has no need of them—it is a great relief.

SYGNE (*with irony*): You are hard, George.

COÛFONTAINE: I fall into line, the rest concerns no one.

SYGNE: In the name of these two innocent ones! Forgive her in the name of these innocent ones!

Consider how young she was, and how terrible it is to die.

Ah, to be a beautiful young woman is more intoxicating than wine!

Tell me that you have forgiven her.

COÛFONTAINE: I no longer think about it.

SYGNE: But say you have forgiven her!

COÛFONTAINE: He who loves much does not easily forgive.

SYGNE: My heart is breaking with compassion for you.

COÛFONTAINE: It is only the nights that are bad, but sleep always comes at length when one is tired.

SYGNE: And they are all three dead!

COÛFONTAINE: Spare me, Sygne, and try to be calmer.

SYGNE: O God, so all that I have done is useless and vain!

COÛFONTAINE: That is the last word on all our efforts. But in your case it is to God that you say it.

SYGNE: "My generation has been rolled up and taken away from me like the shepherd's tent!"

Long ago I saw my father and mother, and your father and mother, Coûfontaine, stand on the scaffold together,

Those saintly faces looking down at us, all four bound like victims, our fathers and mothers who were struck down one after another beneath the axe!

And when it was my mother's turn, the executioner, winding her grey hair around his wrist, dragged her head under the knife.

We were in the first row and you held my hand, and their blood spurted out over us.

I saw it all and did not faint, and afterwards we returned home on foot.

Man cut down the tree, and God now remembers us and is taking away the fruit.

O God, Thou hast singled out the few possessions we still had. Thy will be done! Thy bitter will, Thy bitter will . . .

We alone remain, George, you and I,

You and I alone, more and more one in spirit, and life itself shrinks away from us,

In a world in which we have ceased to have lot or share.

COÛFONTAINE: You must keep away from me and work out your own happiness.

SYGNE: It is I now who hold your hand, as you held mine that May morning.

COÛFONTAINE: You are young and rich, and life lies beautiful before you.

SYGNE: That is what the bells sang on your wedding day.

COÛFONTAINE: It is not the song I heard.

SYGNE: I know you received the sacrament, an unbeliever.

COÛFONTAINE: I did not believe. I knew all beforehand.

But I was a prisoner, as one who could do no otherwise.

SYGNE: And the poor child loved you.

COÛFONTAINE: I was like the miner leaving his mine for a moment and perceiving that it is the month of April after all.

With what a foolish thirst for happiness I was suddenly seized!

SYGNE: You had your hour.

COÛFONTAINE: Nay, I did not have it. It did not mistake me for someone else.

SYGNE: What parted you then?

COÛFONTAINE: The blood of my father on my face.

SYGNE: And that blood also on your hands?

COÛFONTAINE: Does it horrify you, Sygne?

SYGNE: Alas, may God forgive me, it does not horrify me!

COÛFONTAINE: Yet it is the blood of many innocent people.

Remember the street of Saint-Nicaise.[1]

SYGNE: Have you not paid for it with your own?

COÛFONTAINE: It is true. O my wife and my poor children!

SYGNE: I am still left.

COÛFONTAINE: A girl whose name will one day change.

SYGNE: But my name has been confirmed to me by a second baptism.

COÛFONTAINE: I shared that sacrament with you.

SYGNE: Not unworthily that time.

O George, all our race on that day was pressed in the wine-press.

COÛFONTAINE: O sacred wine flowing from that fourfold heart!

SYGNE: Their blood was mingled with mine.

COÛFONTAINE: The old stem gives us its sap no more.

[1] Royalist attempt to murder Napoleon.

SYGNE: There remains a pure wine! The name lives in us.

COÛFONTAINE: O soul like unto my soul! O my strange twin sister!

You understand these things.

As the earth gives us her name so I give her what is human in me.

In her we have our roots, in me who by God's grace am her lord, she has her fruit.

That is why I, with my title of nobility, bear her name better than others.

My fief, like a small France, is my kingdom, the earth in me and my line becomes gentle and noble, like some rare thing which may not be purchased.

And just as the honey or flowers or wine that she produces

Or as the game that is shot there, or the cattle that graze there, can be recognised among all others,

So, among many tender plants, was the Tree-Dormant,

The great Coûfontaine oak which stood in the court of our château,

Whose roots, as they appeared on the day it was uprooted, more entwined than those of the fig-trees I saw on the Coromandel, or than the flowing veins of a young mother's breasts,

Were half buried in the black mortar of the
Roman substructure

Half piercing the compact clay in the native bed
of quartz the colour of the chestnut blossom.

And just as the wine of Bouzy is not that of
Esseaume, so was I born Coûfontaine by natural
law, which the *Droits de l'Homme*[1] cannot
affect.

So the nation, protected against idle dreams, did
not have to make her own chiefs and laws,

But Nature throughout France gave her them,
with her other fruits, good or evil, from king
to judge,

At the curve of every valley, on the slope of every
hill, each one blossoming in due season from
root or stump,

Like flowers and fruits in their variety.

SYGNE (*raising her head and looking at him
steadily*) : Of what moment is all this, George?

COÛFONTAINE: Of what moment?

SYGNE: God willed it. It is well. It is no fault of
ours. Of what avail is it to sulk and quarrel
with Him?

COÛFONTAINE: God Himself cannot take from me
what is mine.

---

[1] "The Rights of man and of the citizen" the name given to the
ensemble of principles adopted by the French National Assembly on
August 4, 1789, as the necessary basis of all human institutions.

SYGNE: Nothing is ours, everything belongs to
Him Who is the Lord enthroned.
And doubtless He cannot take anything from us,
but He can remove us
From the position in which He placed us.

COÛFONTAINE: What am I without the place
whence I get my name?

SYGNE: A man from whom nothing more can be
taken.

COÛFONTAINE: There is one thing at least which
I do not take back after giving.

SYGNE: What is that, George?

COÛFONTAINE (*holding out his hand*): My right
hand.

SYGNE (*giving hers to him*): Nor I this hand that
I give you, brother!

COÛFONTAINE: The world has grown smaller, but
we two remain.

SYGNE (*in a low voice*): *Coûfontaine, adsum.*

COÛFONTAINE: You are my land and my fief, my
share and my heritage,
You are abiding and true
In the place of that false woman who is dead, and
of those children, and of the land.

SYGNE: God alone is true.

COÛFONTAINE (*in an ambiguous tone*): We shall
see presently.

SYGNE: Do not oppose His will.

COÛFONTAINE: What do we know of it?
When the only means we have of learning it is to
act contrary to it.
SYGNE: George, brother! These words are just
like you!
COÛFONTAINE: Since we must be condemned,
Let us make sure of it.
And do not you take sides against me.
SYGNE: What do you intend to do?
COÛFONTAINE: Force
Your God to answer me clearly,
And make Him show at last whether He is on
one side or the other!
SYGNE: O George, what is plainer to be seen than
a thief, and what more do you wish to know?
Happy is he who has something to give, for from
him who has not shall be taken even that which
he has.
Happy is he who is unjustly despoiled, for he has
nothing more to fear from justice.
He who does not accept evil, how shall he receive
good? Thus do I see you cut off from every-
thing, poor brother!
And to me, because I accepted all, behold everything has been restored.
COÛFONTAINE: My concern is not for myself.
Let Coûfontaine perish so long as the King is
restored with France!

SYGNE: So much pain, so many sacrifices, so many
dangers, so much courage and contriving,
So much money, so much blood poured out, your
own blood and that of many others,
And all in vain!
As for me, all my work was finished and the land
restored,
And behold it worthless on my hands!

COÛFONTAINE: It is no use grieving.

SYGNE: I do not grieve, but rejoice!
O God, I rejoice bitterly in Thy grandeur and my
own inutility, and I rejoice that Thou hast
remembered even me in these Thy designs
which surpass all human understanding!
I am a widow, an orphan without relatives, a virgin, and Thou takest away my little ones and
dost mock at me, leaving me alone in the midst
of these lands I have restored.
What could I do else, and was I to fold my arms?
I was a woman, discerning my immediate task,
trying to do good to those who are nearest me,
And I have no wit to imagine anything better, but
whatever I knew to be good I tried to do and
to repair.
So much effort and hardship, poverty, above all,
fear, solitude, old Suzanne's severity towards
me. . . .

COÛFONTAINE: Poor little Sygneau!

SYGNE: . . . The value of every coin harshly
learnt, farthings, halfpennies, crowns, and the
beautiful heavy sovereigns at length, the accounts made clear every night without blot or
erasure,

The value of every field studied, and of each
corner of every field, the price of corn and wine,
of building stone, plaster and wood, and the
labor of men and women,

The value of the old domain learnt by heart, as
much as our grandfather was wont to risk in a
night at cards,

Sales attended, days on horseback or in a cart, in
the heat of the sun or in the cold rain, clad in
my big shepherdess' cloak,

Long hours of contention in lawyers' offices, where
one fights well disguised, with a smiling face,

As in olden times my ancestors fought with visors
lowered and shields pressed to their bodies,

I, a poor girl among those men of law, like Joan
of Arc among the men of war!

Visits to the prefect, discussions with farmers and
contractors,

With a vigilant mind, an open eye, a spirit re-
strained yet inflexible,

Everything at last restored and readjusted (with
the exception of our destroyed château), even

the silver plate and books bearing our arms, piece by piece brought back,

And now behold, with the whole reconstructed, it remains lifeless, like a dismembered corpse whose parts have been joined together again!

COÛFONTAINE: All this has made possible the retreat where I lie hidden to-day,

I and the capture I have made.

SYGNE: Our château has been destroyed, but the holy dwelling still stands,

The wall has been cast down, the moat filled in, the *Tree-Dormant* uprooted,

The well has been polluted, the tower fell with one crash like a man who falls upon his face, the heart of the home has been burst asunder and destroyed,

And of all the old walls there remains only a single gable and the cellar, the refuge of the fox and the hedgehog!

But as for the old abbey growing out of the soil by faith, the mystical dwelling whose seed was the consecrated host,

Since nobody chose it for his own, as Saint John received Our Lady, it is here that I have retired with God,

I, a feeble creature alone beneath the vast arches, a woman with a faint whisper where was once

42

the mighty chorus of those hundred chanting
men of God!

COÛFONTAINE (*looking at the cross*) : That is not
the cross of the monastery?

SYGNE: Do you not recognize it?

It is the bronze crucifix given by our ancestor
Agénor V, the Leaguer,[1]

To replace the old stone one the heretics had cast
down,

The cross on the high road, planted at the junction
of the two royal roads of Rheims and Soissons.

And once more the Republicans rooted it up,
undermining the whole calvary at a single blow,

The cross and the four old lime trees which shaded
it, the only shelter for the harvesters in the open
plain.

And they planted this poor tree of Liberty[2] in its
place, which a single summer dried up into a
mere stick.

The bronze figure was broken in pieces, but it was
not melted into cannon nor made into copper
coins,

And I found the limbs scattered about, as is told
in Plutarch of Isis and Osiris,

The legs broken like those of the thief on the
Cross, the chest used as an anvil by the smith,

[1] The Catholic League formed to crush Protestantism.
[2] Planted widely in 1789 to mark the era of liberty.

The arms preserved by two pious old maids, and
the head at the back of the baker's oven;
And Suzanne and I, walking barefoot a whole
night long,
Carried back the sacred head in our arms, reciting
our prayers,
And now the large and blackened image, worn by
sun and rain, the shamefully crucified,
Is here with us between these walls, hidden from
men, and we are beginning again with it like
exiles
Who make for themselves a hearth with two
brands laid crosswise.

COÛFONTAINE (*his eyes on the cross*): What wood
is that of which the cross is made, which bears
traces of fire?

SYGNE: I made the cross of the beams from our
house.

COÛFONTAINE: The stem is of oak and the cross
piece of chestnut.
It is wood which has now disappeared from this
region,
And yet the framework of our old farms every-
where, and the "timbers" of Rheims Cathedral
are made of it.

SYGNE: But this wood of which the cross is made
will never fail.

COÛFONTAINE: Happy is this tree which bears upon it the weight of a God, or even of a man,

Behold, all that is left of my house, now that I return home,

The beam and the joist in the form of a cross, even that hast Thou taken for Thyself, O Carpenter's Son! and there is no room for two.

And as for me, my proscribed name is replaced by a cross. All my possessions have fallen from me like a garment, and I stand alone in that new state with an unchangeable body and mind,

Cut off, despoiled, inflexible, fruitless!

But now that I return to my country, as did the prodigal son to the home of his father who shared with him his substance,

There is no one to fall on my neck, neither father nor mother,

Neither child nor wife, for all have gone from me.

SYGNE: But I at least, George, I at least am left!

COÛFONTAINE (*looking at her*): Would you consent to wed me, cousin?

SYGNE: O George, I am enough to you without that!

COÛFONTAINE: True. We are too much alike. Nothing new can spring from us.

SYGNE: Who then will continue our race?

COÛFONTAINE: You are young and rich. Keep

these things you have gathered together, they would be of no use to a man cut off from life.

Someone will come.

SYGNE: Do not jest in this way.

COÛFONTAINE: Some handsome hunter with a red beard,

Some young warlike madcap, who will take this perfidious green-eyed Judith from me by the hand,

This Saint Theology who holds a meeting of the Chapter all alone in this monastic place,

This maid exceeding mild, whose modest smile does not stir the corners of her mouth

Enough to make three lines the finest point could trace;

O Sygne, who laughs between these little lines!

And he will take from me for ever my cousin of the forest, the laurel of Dormant, the *"virgo admirabilis"!*

SYGNE: I did not think that you had looked at me so closely!

COÛFONTAINE: I have not. No more than one looks at or listens to oneself. But then you were a part of me.

What did I know of you, Sygne? except that good little hand in mine on the fête of Saint-Jean,

And, later, your clear features, outlined before me

like the plan of a church, accurately drawn with rule and compass,

And again your hand on my head in nights of fever, when I was wounded, ill and pursued,

Or again your brow beneath the lamp when despatches were being sealed and piles of gold were counted.

SYGNE: I am she who stays and is always here.

COÛFONTAINE: Ah, from head to foot you are Coûfontaine, and I can talk with you, and there is not one feature of you and your manner of life that I do not understand!

And you have but to turn your head and there are as many likenesses of our race in you as there were once portraits in the picture gallery of the château.

SYGNE: Therefore I will not give to another that which is of Coûfontaine alone.

COÛFONTAINE: Only those things which are dead and vanquished and impossible are mine.

SYGNE: But I am not dead, George, I am not vanquished, and I am not impossible!

COÛFONTAINE: There is this difference: you are under thirty and I am over forty. We do not belong to the same age.

I am the lopped and branchless trunk, and I see in your brown eyes the freshness of the young leaf.

We do not cast our shadows in the same direction,
    yours draws you forward,
Mine is bound to my heels and I can see nothing
    in front of me that is mine.

SYGNE: Let me renounce the future then!
Let me take an oath like a new knight! O my
    lord! My elder brother! Let me swear to you
Like a nun who takes her vow!
Male of my race! O last and chief of my people!
    I will not leave you without a witness.
The soil betrays us, our strength has been taken,
    but the faith of man in man
Remains, the pure soul finding its leader and
    recognising his colours!
Coûfontaine, I am yours! Take and make of me
    what you will,
Whether I be your wife, or whether, beyond this
    mortal life in the place where the body no
    longer is,
Our souls weld without alloy the one into the
    other!

COÛFONTAINE: Sygne, you whom I found the last
    of all, do not deceive me like the rest. Is it
    possible that I at length shall have
Some sure thing of my own apart from my will?
For since I left this place, while still a child, I
    have had nothing under me but sea,

The sea that is of brine and the sea that is of men; and that false thing in my arms, a treacherous sea likewise. All now is gone.

There was first Monsieur d'Ajac who was a cadet with me on the "Saint-Esprit,"—(How we used to chat in the dark watches of the night while the swell swung our hammocks one against the other!),

I saw him cut in two before my eyes by a cannon-ball.

And then, those I held most sacred—it was the turn of my father and mother, as also of yours, Sygne.

I saw them killed like animals, the blood of their bodies spurted on my face, and I breathed its vapour.

The King who was my king, and the rights which were mine,

That woman who was my right, those children who were my own, even the name I bear and the land with its fief,

They all lied to me, they have all gone, and the very place where these things were is no more.

And I lead this life of a hunted beast, without a safe hiding place, ever in ambush or crouching low, a dangerous and pursued man, threatening and threatened.

And I recall the words of the Hindoo monks—
that all this evil life

Is but a vain shadow, and that it remains with us
only because we move with it,

And that it would be sufficient for us simply to sit
down and wait,

For it to pass us by.

But these are mean temptations; as for me in this
universal ruin

I remain the same, honour and duty the same.

But as for you, Sygne, think what you say. Do
not fail like the others, at this hour when I
am nearing my end.

Do not deceive me who truly hunger and thirst
for your heart which is something outside of me,
and for the loyalty in your heart which is something outside of me,

And not for a thing which is sure, but for one
which is infallible.

SYGNE: God alone is infallible.

COÛFONTAINE: God once more! Leave Him
where He is. We shall see about Him later on.

We shall know, too, later on where He stands
with us.

For if He is so anxious to remain hidden, why did
He leave us a hostage?

SYGNE: I do not understand your words.

(A slight sound of a bell tinkling.

50

COÛFONTAINE: What is that?

SYGNE: It is the priest who has come to say mass as he promised.

COÛFONTAINE: You did wrong to involve him in our affairs.

SYGNE: May the Host he now elevates on the altar hear our words!

He Who gives Himself in the Host, and cannot take Himself back,

To us also has given this sacrament of sacrifice that knows no reservation.

Accept, take with you all that belongs to your race and name,

And to Coûfontaine at least let not Coûfontaine be faithless.

COÛFONTAINE: I accept, Sygne, and add you to the stake of this game I am playing.

O woman, the last of my race, pledge yourself as you desire to do, and receive from your lord the pledge according to the ancient form.

Coûfontaine, receive my glove!

(*He gives her his glove.*

SYGNE: I accept it, George, and you shall never take it back from me.

(*Pause.*

COÛFONTAINE (*raising his finger*): Everything is about to be decided. Our fate is being weighed with that of the whole world.

Violence is reaching its consummation, and the masses with the man of the earth
Are finding again their level.

SYGNE: I know nothing of politics. I have been told that the Pope is no longer in Rome.

COÛFONTAINE: And do you know where he is?

SYGNE: I do not know.

COÛFONTAINE: Here, under this very roof and behind this wall.

(As if deeply moved.

Cæsar is on one side but I have captured the man of God for ours.

—Now leave us, for we have to speak together.

(She goes out.

Act One: Scene Two

A servant has opened the shutters and the whole of the room is seen. Dawn.

There is a high wind and it is pouring in torrents. The violently driven rain streams down the panes. Large trees, whose branches almost touch the windows, darken the room. At intervals is heard the harsh creak of a rusty weathercock. A shaggy-haired dog is lying at the entrance.

Suddenly a panel in the library wainscot slides back, revealing for a moment a secret door which stands open. At the back is seen through it the flame of a candle and the corner of an altar with its altar cloth and mass book upon it.

An old man in a black cassock enters, his head covered with a white skull cap.

POPE PIUS: My son, peace be with you. It is I.
> (COÛFONTAINE, *who was standing, musing, at one of the windows, turns round quickly and kneels before the old man, who gives him his hand to kiss.*

COÛFONTAINE (*rising*): Eat and drink, Holy Father, for the road hither was long and rough, and your rest short before this morning mass.

POPE PIUS: What bread is this that you would give me to eat?

COÛFONTAINE: It is loyal bread. A Christian dwelling shelters you.

POPE PIUS: I recognised an ecclesiastical building.

COÛFONTAINE: This is the Cistercian abbey of Coûfontaine, which my ancestors founded and supported.

My cousin

Sygne bought it with a dispensation,—the château of Dormant having been burnt,—

To keep it from destruction, guarding it for its rightful owners.

POPE PIUS: She is that pious young woman to whom I gave the sacrament last night?

COÛFONTAINE: And I am Viscount Ulysses Agénor George de Coûfontaine et Dormant, Lord Lieutenant of King Louis in France for Champagne and Lorraine.

POPE PIUS: What is the meaning of this violent course? Why have you taken me from my prison?

COÛFONTAINE (*drawing a paper from his pocket*): An order signed by the Emperor. It was I who took upon myself the duty of carrying it out,

The bearer finding himself prevented.

54

All was done in order. Moscow is far away.
Why, who would not honour such a signature?
An absolutely blank cheque valid throughout the
Empire. Everybody obeyed me as if I were
an angel from heaven.

> (*He gives the paper to the Pope who reads
> it silently and returns it.*

Thus I alone have taken Peter from his prison.

POPE PIUS: I thank you, my son.

COÛFONTAINE: You are safe here. Who would
come to look for you in this corner of Marne?

Here is an old dwelling-place, hidden and soli-
tary,

With secret ways leading out through the woods
to three roads and two valleys,

Full of hiding places and exits.

I have used them many times in this struggle I
am carrying on.

POPE PIUS: We are now your prisoner.

COÛFONTAINE: Yes, Father, the prisoner of your
son.

And I say to you like Jacob when he held the
angel so firmly:

I will not let you go till you have blessed me.

POPE PIUS: Poor child! You see that We are a
difficult capture.

COÛFONTAINE: It is God Himself Who gives you
to the King of France.

POPE PIUS (*turning gravely towards the crucifix*) :
Ave, Domine Jesu.

COÛFONTAINE: That is Notre-Seigneur-de-devant-Rheims, and the King took off his hat to it when he went to be crowned.

POPE PIUS: What news is there of the great world?

For no sound has reached Us in Our prison.

COÛFONTAINE: The Usurper is at Moscow.

In all the world there is no sound but the tramp of the armies on the highways and the rumbling of wheels rolling eastward.

Yonder it is said there has been I know not what,

Cities of wood devoured by flames, a victory vaguely won. Europe is empty and nobody speaks on the whole earth.

The world waits in suspense like a man exhausted, overcome.

POPE PIUS: And it is in Moscow that the Emperor has found time to think of an old man like Us?

COÛFONTAINE: You embody God's protest amid the silence of all men.

POPE PIUS: What is this fortress of Joux of which your letter speaks?

COÛFONTAINE: A casemate in the snows whence there is no escape.

POPE PIUS: It has pleased God to pluck Us out of the enemy's hand.

COÛFONTAINE: And then
  Some conclave will meet under the threat of bayo-
    nets,
  Some Cardinal Fesch or Maury[1]
  Will be made pope,—as he has made his brothers
    kings,—
  Chaplain to the Great Emperor.
POPE PIUS (*raising his finger*):   On the roads of
  Judea there were men possessed of devils who
  as soon as they saw our Lord threw themselves
  before Him weeping and crying out.
  And while pursuing Him with insults and stones
  they did not stop repeating: Jesus of Nazareth,
  why persecutest Thou us?
  Even so through all the ages have unholy men
  dealt with Christ's Vicar.
  There has been no peace for men since He appeared among them as one destitute.
  They make their little pacts of a day among themselves, calling them laws, societies, constitutions,
  states, kingdoms,
  According to the power which is given to them
  for a day, and which is good and blessed in
  itself,
  And they think they have determined the progress
  of the world, moulding all things for eternity
  according to their will,

[1] Creatures of Napoleon.

And because they know not exactly what share to
give Him, they grow angry with God,
Who desires no share.

> (*He turns gravely towards the crucifix.*

He is naked and nothing belongs to Him.

> (*Silence.*

And they would arrest and imprison Him with
rules and barriers, with liberties and concordats.
And Our duty is to lend Ourselves to their whim,
like a fisherman on the sea who makes the best
of the weather, having no choice,
For the good of men's souls, as far as is permissible.
—And as for this Emperor of today, he is like a
spoiled child who is thwarted.
He pretends to be master, not knowing he is one
of my poor children like all the rest.
The Conqueror of men, as he calls himself, behold
him to-day seeking to bind and to force God,
to get God on his side, taking His Vicar as
hostage.
Not understanding why it has pleased the Almighty to choose His representative from
among the feeblest on earth,
Even this old man whose food is a little honey
and fish, this poor foolish priest who knows
nought save his catechism.
And because he knows not what to give Us, behold
him taking from Us even that which we have,

The goods in our charge, the vine of Naboth, the
patrimony of Peter, even the fisherman's ring
on Our finger,
So that on earth our Lord is again without refuge
as in the days of Galilee, and in His own house
is as a captive and as one merely tolerated;
And even Our life: as if that were still living
which was buried with Christ.

> (*Violent gust of wind which shakes the
> house. Whistling and howling. A sheet
> of water pours down the panes of the four
> windows. The* POPE *shivers and wraps
> himself more tightly in his cloak, looking
> round him with terror.*

COÛFONTAINE: This is not the sunshine of Tivoli
nor the breeze of Mount Sabin.

POPE PIUS: A wild place for a young woman to
live alone.

COÛFONTAINE: She has a roof over her head and
this place is her own.
I do not see what she can ask for more.
Would to heaven that I might always be dry at
night and that I might have the good soil of my
own land ever beneath my feet!
—This is our September downpour, which sweeps
over the harvest fields and softens the earth for
tillage.

> (*A fresh gust of wind.*

POPE PIUS (*in a low tone*): Pray ye that your
flight be not in the winter, neither on the Sab-
bath day.

COÛFONTAINE (*musing*): This recalls old times,
when the great monsoons of Pondicherry rid
us of the English frigates.

POPE PIUS: Where are the former masters of this
house?

COÛFONTAINE: They have not left it, they have not
violated the cloister.

They are laid side by side in good order, feet
together, in the convent garden, the six priests,
the eight novices, and the twelve lay-brothers,

The abbot in the centre with the prior on his right
and all the others according to the date of their
vows.

By the grace of my foster-brother, a former novice
of theirs who directed their execution,

In the year of grace one thousand seven hundred
and ninety-three,

Toussaint Turelure, son of Quiriace the wood-
cutter and sorcerer, now baron of the Empire
and prefect of Marne,

Within whose domain I have led your Holiness.

POPE PIUS: We will go and pray over the remains
of these martyrs.

(*The dog raises its head and stands with its
forepaws against one of the windows.*

60

COÛFONTAINE: Lie down, lie down, Sylla!
> What is the matter with my dog of noble line?   Is
> it my brother Toussaint's name which makes
> you silently show your teeth like that?
> Who would come to us here in such a storm?
>> (*He listens.   The dog drops again on its
>> paws.*

COÛFONTAINE (*pointing to the table which is laid*) :
> Eat, Holy Father.
>> (*The* POPE *sits down at the table.*   COÛFON-
>> TAINE *stands respectfully at his side, serv-
>> ing him.   The dog has lain down again
>> in a corner.*

COÛFONTAINE: The beast has a bad temper and we
> mustn't play with her.
> It is I who taught her to be quiet.
> We have spent together many hours, many days,
> and many intervals without knowledge of the
> flight of time (when I even stopped my watch
> on account of its noise),
> Crouched in some dangerous corner, in some dark
> room,
> Nothing with me but this beast, poor, obscure, and
> faithful.
> Myself becoming almost a beast, as she almost an
> aristocrat.
>> (*Pause.*
> We know what perpetual danger is.
>> (*He muses.*

61

Therein have I understood my ancestors, the scattered seigniors of our estates and of our Merovingian domains.

They subsisted on the poor verminous soil which was ravaged by rabbits and boars, and on the patch of black earth, full of stumps, which they sowed, still hot, like a cake, from the fire that cleared it.

Like a fish in a hidden pool, like a spider in its sticky web,

They spent day and night listening, on the alert for man and game, ambushed in the fresh and trembling verdure, enveloped in mist,

Which carried odours and sounds to them like a subtile fluid.

> (*The* POPE, *having finished eating, rises and makes the sign of the cross.*

POPE PIUS: *Deo gratias!* I thank you, son, for this meal.

COÛFONTAINE: A rude welcome for the greatest king of the earth!

But here at least you are far from the Count of Chabrol, and from the noble Borghèse and the Christian Portalis.[1]

Your Holiness will have peace for a few days.

POPE PIUS: Where do you wish to take me?

---

[1] Ecclesiastical ministers of Napoleon.

COÛFONTAINE: To England, where the King of France is.

POPE PIUS: My son, do not unto Us the wrong of delivering the Pope into the hands of heretics.

COÛFONTAINE: It is on their account that you are here, refusing to be divided from them.[1]

POPE PIUS: It is true. Why then should I consent to be put under the interdict of my own children?

COÛFONTAINE: Does not prison separate you from them?

POPE PIUS: Where the Cross is, there the Church dies not.

COÛFONTAINE: Come and be free.

POPE PIUS: I do not desire freedom among the dead.

COÛFONTAINE: Where can I take you where Cæsar is not?

POPE PIUS: Where Peter is, over whose bones I in turn am Peter.

COÛFONTAINE: To Rome you say?
Your place is taken there by a prefect.

POPE PIUS: On the earth, but not under it where I can wait. Let the Catacombs receive anew the salvation of all men!

Three centuries the Church did wait. And cannot I wait three days with Christ?

---

[1] The Pope's lands were still open to English commerce.

COÛFONTAINE: Leave Rome and recover the world.

POPE PIUS: Where the foundation is, there is Peter.

COÛFONTAINE: In his old age Peter's hands were bound and he was led whither he did not wish to go.

POPE PIUS: My child, here are Our hands, and blessed be he that cometh in the name of the Lord!

COÛFONTAINE: Why is it your will only to yield to force, when love calls you?

POPE PIUS: The other will of that Church whose eternal husband I am, holds me back.

COÛFONTAINE: Shall the rock of the world only serve to strengthen Cæsar?

POPE PIUS: That it was against which the foot of the heterogeneous idol was broken.

COÛFONTAINE: Holy Father, are you with us or against us?

POPE PIUS: A question I heard often at Savona.

COÛFONTAINE: But we are the sons who have remained faithful, what recompense have we for our obedience?

POPE PIUS: O eldest son, what have We to give you? for the prodigal son has taken everything from Us.

COÛFONTAINE: Indeed, Father, old age must have
    dimmed your sight
Since you have blessed the goats instead of the
    sheep.

POPE PIUS: Could I not anoint such a head
When Jesus Himself kissed the feet of Judas?

COÛFONTAINE: Holy Father, let me talk with you,
    and explain all.
Since you are here and I have you with me, God's
    Vicar,
For like a young man who speaks to his father
    confessor once a year, I have much to say to you.
And, besides, do you not belong to us all? and a
    single ewe is as much to you as all the others
    together.
And I do not confess every day: the life I live is
    not that of a nun. When the King comes back,
    it will be time then to put on the clean shirt.
—Why do you offend us even as God?
He humiliates the good and exalts the wicked.
    Those are His ways and we can say nothing to
    Him.
But you are human. You are capable of speech,
    and have you nothing to answer us? Or whom
    shall we question?
What is good or evil for us, is it not the same for
    the Pope? and does success make any differ-
    ence?

Is it good that a man should take what does not
belong to him?

And this brigand who has taken Rome from you,
has he not taken France from his King?

POPE PIUS: The world may go on without a king,
but not without the Pope.

COÛFONTAINE: Can it go on without right? and is
right concerned with what a man has or with
what he has not?

POPE PIUS: Man has nothing which is not from
God alone.

COÛFONTAINE: Then is not what he has very
sacred? To be and to have are the first two
verbs from which all others are made.

What we possess is called *the good*.

Man has nothing which is not from God alone,
and which he does not dispose of entirely.

According to the way of the donor, God having
done nothing

Without man to complete and preserve the gift,
in such a manner

That it does not exist except as it exists for man.

And he who cannot preserve the good, let another
take it from him,

As Louis occupies the seat of Charles and of
Clovis: about that I make no complaint.

POPE PIUS: And as this newcomer is seated in the
place left vacant.

COÛFONTAINE: But he is not seated; you see him uneasy and standing!

Holy Father, it is not against a man that I am come to ask your thunderbolt

But against all these new rights, for are a man's rights concerned with what he has, or with what he has not?

You have heard with horror the doctrine

That every man has equal rights by his own nature,

And the rights of others become merely a wrong that is done him.

Thus one can no longer make a free gift, and there is nothing free among men.

Is that also approved by God?

POPE PIUS: Is it to put such questions to a poor old man that you have pounced upon me like an eagle?

COÛFONTAINE: Give answer, you who have authority, for it is hard to do one's duty in the dark.

POPE PIUS: Duty is concerned with the things at hand, about which there is no doubt.

COÛFONTAINE: What is nearer to me in the night than my own thought?

A hunted man thinking alone in a ditch the whole night long—

A whole night of thinking in the rain brews a muddy drink!

POPE PIUS: We must tell Our beads when sleep
   does not come and not add the night
Unto the day whereof the evil is sufficient.

COÛFONTAINE: I have beads to tell in my heart
   when I cannot sleep, bead by bead,
The severed heads of my father and mother and
   all my kin.
We alone survive, Sygne and I.

POPE PIUS: Why do you speak then of your night
   when you have such bright lights in it?

COÛFONTAINE: They show us the end and not the
   road.

POPE PIUS: Take no thought for many things
   when one alone is sufficient,
But consider those beautiful heavenly lilies which
   toil not neither do they spin.

COÛFONTAINE: Are the earthly ones withered for
   ever?

POPE PIUS: That is known by the earth which holds
   their roots.

COÛFONTAINE: But I, so long as I live, must toil
   and must spin my thread,
And lo, I have no longer my earth under me, and
   the world to which I belong has been taken
   from me,
Wherein of all my line was continued in me the
   mission to serve while commanding.

I look around and there is no longer a society of
men,

But only the "law," as it is called, and the machine-
printed text, the inanimate will, a vain idol.

Where there are rights there is no longer love.

The law of God was hard from which Christ set
us free. How much harder will be the law of
man?

Can a society continue in which every man believes it exists at the expense of his own rights?

As you see with this man, as soon as he has taken
one thing he is obliged to take all the rest,

To reconquer the world every instant in order
to make a single step safe.

POPE PIUS: We have no permanent dwelling
place here.

COÛFONTAINE: Is it not our duty, however, to seek
out and maintain the best in everything?

Is it not written that all power comes from God?
therefore it comes not from man.

I compare it not to a sword, but to a balm with
which the head is anointed and the whole body
suffused.

That is why our kings were consecrated, like
bishops, to rule over France,

Consecrated on the brow with the bishops' holy oil,
receiving the sacrament in both kinds,

Anointed with a precious ointment on their shoulders and their arms,
Ordained for command, which is force tempered with gentleness.
Has the sacred phial no longer any authority?

POPE PIUS: You know, since you saw the blessed king die.

COÛFONTAINE: A king's virtue is not shown by his death.

POPE PIUS: But a saint is more in God's sight than many kings and thrones.

COÛFONTAINE: Is not one of the petitions in the Lord's prayer we repeat every day that the kingdom may come?

POPE PIUS: Therefore it has not yet come.

COÛFONTAINE: Do not all things take substance before us?

POPE PIUS: The substance of this world passes away.

COÛFONTAINE: But will that of God pass away?

POPE PIUS: It passes not away so long as the cross endures.

COÛFONTAINE: Father! Father!
The age of faith is dead,
Faith in God, the faith of vassal in liege.
The King is God's image to whom alone may be given the obedience due unto Him.

Now again begins the servitude of man to man,
imposed by superior force and by law,

As it was in the days of Tiberius,—and they call
this liberty.

POPE PIUS: God's image, which has returned to
God,

And from which God is withdrawn, is nothing
more than a pagan idol.

COÛFONTAINE: Nevertheless a king is a man; the
abstract idea is the pure idol,

The tyrant established for ever, a thing wrought
by man not by nature.

These men of the law think all is ordered by con-
tract!

POPE PIUS (*in a low tone*): Taking back that old
parchment which was fastened to the cross.

COÛFONTAINE: What do you say? I do not hear
you.

POPE PIUS: And We scarcely see you. It is dark
in this library. We are old, my son, and Our
sight is poor.

But you are a young man, and you are free, having
neither wife nor children,

Accustomed to the wide horizon your feet carry
you boldly whithersoever your eyes see,

But We, the high priest, who carry all peoples
on Our heart day and night like the stones of
the ancient breastplate,

Are not permitted the rapid pace.

It is not the light of reason which guides Us, but that of conscience,

A feeble flame, a patient glimmer,

Which shows Us not what is expedient but what is necessary, not the future but the present.

COÛFONTAINE: Come with me. Withdraw yourself from the world.

Render unto Cæsar for a time this cowardly world which accepts the coin of Cæsar.

POPE PIUS: I cannot excommunicate myself from the universe.

COÛFONTAINE: Deliver us from our captivity.

POPE PIUS: I can only absolve you.

COÛFONTAINE: Has not all power been given you to bind and to loose?

POPE PIUS: Even Peter could not loose 'himself, he who is called *Es-liens*.[1]

COÛFONTAINE: Is it the light in you which says No?

POPE PIUS: Where Peter is there am I. It is not for the Pope to wander.

COÛFONTAINE: But at Rome you will find constraint again.

POPE PIUS: Force alone absolves me from necessity.

[1] In bonds.

COÛFONTAINE: Must I then employ it myself?

POPE PIUS: It is written: Thou shalt honour thy
father and thy mother.

COÛFONTAINE: Or shall I simply withdraw?
> (*The* POPE *is silent.   Noise of the rain.
> He muses:*

The rain falls,

Effacing with the same patience

The harvest which it has helped to bring to
fruition,

Preparing the earth as a sepulchre, the mighty
burial of seeds.

And as for us, whatever we do, what must be cannot be altered.

> (*Aloud.*

Holy Father, know that it is your cause above all
else which is of moment.

What I have just accomplished is enough for ours:

The violence done to you has been made known,
and at the same time our own good will:

Whether you are now saved or recaptured,

There are advantages either way.
> (*The* POPE *is silent as though he does not
> hear.*

Do you hear me, Holy Father?

POPE PIUS: Did you not say that you would leave
Us here for a few days?

COÛFONTAINE: I do not know exactly how many. I must think and see.

POPE PIUS: Give God time in which to advise us both.

COÛFONTAINE: Your Holiness is very weary?

POPE PIUS: Weary of body, even more weary of soul! Give Us these few days of rest, my son.

It is hard for a poor monk to prefer his own will.

Non meam, Domine. Not mine,

Not mine, Lord, but Thine.

> (*He speaks slowly, as if distraught and absorbed.*
> *Ut quid persequimini me sicut Deus, vos saltem amici mei?*

Why do ye persecute me, my brother bishops?

Cardinals, counsellors of God's Vicar, is it for this that I opened your mouths?

You see that it is not in Our power to do otherwise.

> (*Silence. The* POPE *gradually bows his head over his breast and dozes.*

COÛFONTAINE (*turning towards the crucifix*): Lord God, if perchance Thou dost exist, as my sister Sygne believes, I bring Thee this innocent, who sleeps in Thy arms.

It is no longer a question of Thy remaining hidden; it is Thy concern alone—I have forced Thee to reveal Thyself.

74

The Corsican no longer holds this hostage. I have
  restored the balance of the scales. Therefore
  decide in Thy freedom.
Everything is brought to the light of day.
Everything will appear openly in the sight of
  men and of angels.
As for me, whatsoever Thou doest, I have taken
  precautions.
Since my hand has been rejected, I withdraw it.
If the old man escapes it is I who have saved him.
And if the ogre recaptures him the scandal must
  now be public, and he must tie this millstone
  around his neck.

(*He goes out.*

Act Two: Scene One

The scene as in the first act. Afternoon of the same day. The sun is shining brightly into the room.

SYGNE *and* TURELURE. *The latter is a tall man, slightly lame; his narrow and very hooked nose projects from his forehead without any curve, somewhat like a ram's.*

Coffee is served on a small table.

BARON TURELURE: This good coffee did not grow on an oak tree, and this sugar is too white not to have come from the land of the negroes.

SYGNE: Excuse me. You have taken me unawares. I had no time to get treacle and chicory.

BARON TURELURE: I excuse you!
> (*He speaks thoughtfully, and warms a small glass of brandy in the hollow of his broad hand. He sniffs the brandy from time to time but does not drink it. He takes but one swallow of the coffee.*)

A happy ending to an excellent meal.

Why do you speak to me of an improvised reception? Good heavens!

What a meal for this out-of-the-way place!

My mother left pupils in your kitchen who do her credit.

Poor woman! It's a long time since I have tasted her cooking.

SYGNE: My dear Suzanne!

BARON TURELURE: You will forgive me for not showing any emotion?

All the hatred she had for her husband the blessed woman transferred to me.

A general, a prefect, a baron, Ah, *mon Dieu,* all that hardly dazzled her!

When that daughter of a game-keeper married a poacher, after the first flash of passion, it was bound to end badly.

When the time came we ranged ourselves each on his own side.

And here I am, uniting in myself the love of order and the instinct of precaution,

(*He breathes in the air lightly.*

With the nose of a hound scenting its prey.

SYGNE: Monsieur le Préfet, is it on a police errand then you have come here today?

BARON TURELURE: What a fearful thought! Is anything disturbing ever heard of Coûfontaine?

Everything is quiet in your woods, as in the days of the monks.

No coaches overturned, no tales of priests in hiding. One might say that your presence is a
protection for the whole place.

(*He winks an eye.*

Of course, this visit is only a pretext. Nothing
can be hidden from you.

But what I have to say to you is as awkward as the
devil. Give me time to get it out. How shall
I put it? In a way I have come to ask advice
from you.

And it is always with some emotion that I see
again these places where I spent my youth.

SYGNE: Monsieur le Préfet,
I do not find you nowadays in a monk's dress, with
hands in sleeves and head in hood.

BARON TURELURE: It is a useful dress.
I can see myself yet saying matins before dawn
with the devil of a big hare that I had just
snared hanging quite warm under my scapulary.

That made the fasting life of the monastery more
agreeable to me.

What good hunts I have had at night in these big
woods, on the watch with my old musket!
Nobody will get the better of me here, I know
all the paths.

Yes. The master of the novices was old, and I had
a voice like a trumpet, and looked well in the
choir.

Yet more than once I have confessed my sins in
this very place at the feet of the reverend abbot.

SYGNE: Suzanne never spoke about you to me.

BARON TURELURE: It was her idea that I should
become a monk. It seems I had something or
other to atone for.

My father terrified her with his old wolfish ways,
bête fausse as they say, and his method of curing
sprains while making the sign of the cross over
them with the big toe of his left foot.

Monsieur Badilon must remember him. The
priests at that time

Never said mass without passing their hands under
the altar cloth to make sure that some strange
scrawl had not been put there.

It gave me pleasure to meet Badilon just now.
He's a good companion and on occasion a good
bottle does not frighten him.

I know that you see him often. And yet it's some
distance from the rectory here.

—Nothing has changed, you have restored everything to its place, even all those old books.
There is only this crucifix which does not look
well.

—You made a good bargain at the price that was
told me.

Ah, yes! National property has some good in it.

SYGNE (*meaningly*): It is to you I owe this.

BARON TURELURE: I understand what you mean. And I know everything that is said of me, but it is false.

What is true is quite sufficient. I had them killed for love of my country in the pure enthusiasm of my heart!

I was young and innocent then, and stood firm on my two legs.

You must understand before judging. Ah, it was blood that I had in my veins, the right stuff!

Not pale pumpkin juice, but brandy boiling hot from the still, and gunpowder,

Full of passion, full of ideas, and a heart hard as a flint!

Then the grapeshot which broke my leg made me understand a good deal.

Those good monks! Bless me, I bear them no ill will and thanks to me they are entering into glory and the saints' calendar,

Just like Saint Eloi, and Saint Stapin who cures the belly ache, and whose pictures are seen on the blacksmith's and on the cobbler's walls,

Suddenly lit up by the flames spurting out from beneath the bellows, or by the glow of a pipe lighted from a fagot.

That's better than foolishly working out one's salvation by eating spinach with nut oil! (Vile stuff!)

—And I see again our precentor, climbing into
the lecturn,

Sceptre in hand, glittering with gold like Apollo,
and walking in all his majesty.

And poor me! I shall have my place in the
legend as the good prefect Olibrius.

Well! They are all at rest now along the wall,
between the pumpkins and the Jerusalem arti-
chokes.

SYGNE: You horrify me.

BARON TURELURE: I know. It is on this feeling
that our friendship is built.

SYGNE: But there is no friendship.

BARON TURELURE: There is mutual interest.

SYGNE: But you are the very image of what I
detest.

BARON TURELURE: A pathetic and battered
image!

SYGNE: At least you might hide your soul from me.

BARON TURELURE: How then will you heal it for
me?

SYGNE: The bone is broken, and my simples will
not put you together again.

BARON TURELURE: It is your duty, however, to do
good to me.

SYGNE: A duty towards you?

BARON TURELURE: What is a generation? Was I
not born your serf and your servant's son?

How long have my people served yours?
And will you do nothing for me?

SYGNE: You are a prefect and I am under your administration.

BARON TURELURE: I am a prefect, and do my prefect's duty.

But I am also a cripple, one of those poor wretches who are stubborn and want to hear nothing.

SYGNE: It is but just that you should be a cripple.

BARON TURELURE: It is not right then that you should be here.

SYGNE: What duty have I towards you?

BARON TURELURE: That of all your race towards mine.

SYGNE: Is it we who broke the bond?

BARON TURELURE: It is you, it is we. We served you and you no longer served any purpose.

SYGNE: What have you to ask of me, then?

BARON TURELURE: I am your old Suzanne's son. Do not be so hard with me!

Here I am coming back to my bit of earth like a badger with a broken leg and the other *bêtes fausses*.

I see there are other relations among men than the struggle of each to get the better of the others and to pay his taxes.

Just as the things of nature help one another, and

as certain plants have medicinal virtues for certain beings only,

Why should men not have a natural order among themselves?

Isn't that one of your ideas? You see I'm a good listener.

SYGNE: A little more and you will be a royalist.

BARON TURELURE: Ah, well! I think of a good many things.

The Emperor is risking his all. It is not wholly sound and reasonable.

This Empire he has heaped up is a mass of pillage. It has neither shape, nor measure, nor sense.

And there he is at present in Russia! Issuing a decree about the Comédie Française from the summit of the Sparrow Mountains!

—You know that the Pope has escaped from his residence?

SYGNE: What do we know here in our woods?

BARON TURELURE: The thing is clear. Snatched like a kiss! Carried off like a girl by a dragon. It's an impudent stroke.

There's one hand that I recognise in this.

What care I! The people of Paris are beside themselves, but let them get out of it as they may!

It's not with me that the old man has taken refuge.

SYGNE: May the Holy Father escape from his enemies!

BARON TURELURE: Amen! But at all events I have given one or two little orders.

SYGNE: He will not fall into your hands.

BARON TURELURE: So much the worse for him. He might fall into others less satisfactory.

SYGNE: Do you enjoy this police work?

BARON TURELURE: Not at all, but one must do one's work.

SYGNE: You think yourself powerful and clever, because you sail with wind and current,
But that alone is firm which rests upon what is permanent.

BARON TURELURE: And what is more permanent than change itself?

SYGNE: On it we base our hope.

BARON TURELURE: That which is dead . . .

SYGNE: . . . Produces life.

BARON TURELURE: But life does not re-enter it.

SYGNE: That duty dies not that men owe to one another.

BARON TURELURE: Is this not what we used to call "fraternity"?

SYGNE: It is only in one man that all men can be one.

BARON TURELURE: The son who attains his majority is no longer subject to his father.

SYGNE: But the wife always remains subject to her husband.

BARON TURELURE: We no longer recognise eternal vows.

SYGNE: A sad freedom thus deprived of its royal right!

BARON TURELURE: What do you call royal?

SYGNE: That which makes a king while sacrificing itself.

BARON TURELURE: What do you think of all our plebiscites?

SYGNE: I have a horror of that adulterous Yes.

BARON TURELURE: Shall the dead bind the living for ever?

SYGNE: By our very birth we are compelled to accept a fixed order.

BARON TURELURE: We hold that man is master of himself at all times, master of his own person.

SYGNE: He who is incapable of anything eternal is without faith.

BARON TURELURE: What is more vain than a barren and lifeless marriage?

SYGNE: That oath we have taken with the Bishop of France cannot be cancelled.

BARON TURELURE: We do not recognise it.

SYGNE: He who is not a husband will be a slave. He who will not consent will be constrained.

He who is not a member of the church will be a slave of the law.

BARON TURELURE: Law is reason in writing.

SYGNE: The reason of those who wrote it.

BARON TURELURE: We have proclaimed the right of man to understand.

SYGNE: Who will understand man himself?

BARON TURELURE: What do you mean?

SYGNE: What will bind men together?

BARON TURELURE: Their common interest.

SYGNE: Nature has more remote ends.

BARON TURELURE: Nature once more! Theorist! The storm, like the one which blew last night, is also nature.

It is because the faded thing is no longer necessary that it can live no more. Chance is not nature.

SYGNE: This reason of yours is even less so.

BARON TURELURE: A man is not a plant. Those are insipid comparisons!

Reason is our own nature, which is a superior order.

Understand me a little! Understand at least before despising!

Let me say what there is to be said on my side.

SYGNE: Speak.

BARON TURELURE: I am sure I interest you.

I well know I shall not make you change your

mind, but at least understand me before judging me, merciless one!

And who knows if I am not ready to be converted? Let us settle this question between us.

Besides, it will give us a better topic of conversation than all these rumours about a donkey and a dog!

Your cousin's dog, it seems! A donkey with an old woman on its back, or a priest. There's no sense in it. Everybody knows that George is in England. So much the better for him.

—No.

Was the revolution directed against the King or against God? or against nobles and monks and parliament and all those outlandish bodies? Listen:

It was a revolution against chance!

When a man wishes to put his ruined estate in order,

He does not trouble himself superstitiously about custom and tradition, or simply go on doing what he did before.

He resorts to older things, namely, the earth and the sun,

Trusting in his own reason.

Where is the wrong if also in the Republic, in that encumbered household, we have tried to bring order and logic,

Making a general inventory, a list of all our
organic wants, a declaration of the rights of the
members of the community,

And holding only to those things which are evi-
dent to each one?

SYGNE: Then all will be reduced to interest?

BARON TURELURE: Interest is what draws men
together.

SYGNE: But in no way what unites them.

BARON TURELURE: And what will unite them?

SYGNE: Only the love which has made men will
unite them.

BARON TURELURE: It was a great love that the
king and nobles had for us!

SYGNE: The dead tree still makes good timber.

BARON TURELURE: There's no way of convincing
you! You speak like Pallas herself, in the good
days of the wise bird which is to be seen on her
head.

And it is I who am wrong to speak rationally.

It was hardly a question of reason in the fine sunshine of that beautiful summer of the year One
[of the Republic]! How good were the green-
gages that year—we had only to pluck them—
and how warm it was!

Lord! how young we were then; the world was
not big enough for us!

We were going to pull down all the old lumber;
we were going to make something very much
more beautiful!

We were going to level everything, to lie down
together, to walk without restraint and in the
garb of the revolution in a regenerated universe,
to march through the world we had delivered
from gods and tyrants!

It is also the fault of all those old things which
were not firm on their foundations; it was too
tempting to shake them a little to see what might
happen!

Is it our fault if everything has fallen about us?
'Pon my word I regret nothing.

It was just the same with that fat Louis the Six-
teenth! His head was not very firm on his
shoulders.

Quantum potes, tantum aude! That's the Frenchman's motto.

And as long as there are Frenchmen you will not
deprive them of the old enthusiasm, you will
not deprive them of their old dare-devil spirit
of adventure and invention!

SYGNE: Something of it still survives in you.

BARON TURELURE: 'Pon my word it's true! and
that encourages me to tell you at once what I
came to tell you.

SYGNE: I am not anxious to hear it.

BARON TURELURE: You shall hear it, however.
Mademoiselle Sygne de Coûfontaine,
I love you and I have the honour to ask for your
hand.

SYGNE: You honour me, Monsieur le Préfet.

BARON TURELURE: Good heavens! There's no
need to turn white like this, as if I had struck
you in the face.

SYGNE: You can say anything to me. I have no one
to defend me and must hear all.

BARON TURELURE: It is I, rather, who am in your
power. What have you to fear from this
wretched cripple?

SYGNE: I fear nobody in the world.

BARON TURELURE: I know. How attractive you
are with your sparkling eyes and your tightly
closed smiling mouth, like a person silently
arming himself!
Ah, I know I shall not prevail upon you, and that
you have complete control over yourself!
You are coldness itself, reason itself, and it is just
that which fires my blood, just that which
attracts me and drives me to despair.
Those perfect features and that serene spirit, an
oval-faced angel!
You are self-confident and triumphal; everything
with you has its place assigned; everything is
promptly determined.

Is there no vulnerable place in that politic heart?

Would you not stoop towards a man condemned
to death and take him in your arms in order to
save him!

My body is broken, my soul is in darkness and
towards you I turn my face stained with crime
and despairing!

SYGNE: How dare you speak to me in this way?

BARON TURELURE: I have dared greater things.

If we dared only reasonable things the King would
still be on his throne.

Here am I like the people of Paris when they
flung themselves on the railings of Versailles
with fury, calling for the King and Queen!

SYGNE: Is not their blood and ours sufficient for
you?

BARON TURELURE: I wish to subdue the soul!

It is an army which is being broken that I still
want, the panic of a yielding army that I want
to see in those lovely cold eyes!

SYGNE: You will see nothing of the kind.

BARON TURELURE: I don't know. There must be
an end to this. Here we've lived face to face
for ten years, and, I'm bound to confess it,

It is you who have had the best of it.

You read everything in my eyes, and I never find
your observation at fault.

You get everything from me while I have nothing
from you. Ah! the old slavery of my mother
continues!

I had to speak to you finally. Do not pretend to
look astonished.

SYGNE: Baron, it is true,

I have always found in you a kind and courteous
man.

BARON TURELURE: I did what I could.

SYGNE: Your advice has been valuable to me, your
patronage inestimable.

I reproach myself for having abused it.

BARON TURELURE: The gain has been on both
sides.

SYGNE: Why destroy whatever was possible between us? Let us leave matters as they are. Is
it in my power to be yours?

BARON TURELURE: Sygne,

Is it in my power not to desire you?

SYGNE: Only reasonable things ought to be desired.

BARON TURELURE: Reason consists in making the
best of facts as they are.

And the fact is that I love you, a matter in which
I am powerless.

Nature knows more about these things than you
and I.

And if I love you it is because there is something
in you which must be loved by me.

So I come to you directly. When instincts are so insistent,

There's only one thing for a man to do! It is to take command of them, march at their head, half wheeling to the left about.

SYGNE: But what are your reasons for speaking to me about this today?

BARON TURELURE: They are strong and pertinent.

SYGNE: Allow me time to consider before giving you an answer.

BARON TURELURE: I am sorry, I cannot. You must answer me at once.

Do not try to be shrewder than I.

SYGNE: You know that it is a small thing to say that I do not love you.

BARON TURELURE: Mademoiselle, it is too difficult to know what pleases you.

When we did for the Austrian dogs with our bayonets it did not please them either.

SYGNE (*looking at him*): You are not pleasant to look at.

BARON TURELURE: I am not pleasant but useful. What a predicament you are in! It is heaven, I tell you, which has sent me expressly to save you!

And not you alone. But the fate of your King and of your religion,

And of your cousin himself, this hero out of the past, our bold Agénor.

Who knows but what you hold it at this moment in your delicate fingers?

Do not take me for a fanatic. France first. I'm a practical man.

Let everybody do his duty as I do and we shall succeed!

Even the King himself will not frighten me on the day he makes me a minister.

SYGNE: Why do you speak to me of my cousin George?

BARON TURELURE (*with a thundering voice*): Because he is here, and I have him by the throat.

SYGNE: Take him then if you are capable of it.

BARON TURELURE: Is his fate indifferent to you?

SYGNE: A long time ago we made our compact with death.

BARON TURELURE: What do your cousin and his miserable tomfooleries matter to me?

SYGNE: What do citizen Turelure and his wretched tricks matter to me?

BARON TURELURE: I have better hostages in my hand.

You say nothing.

SYGNE: What do I know of your official speculations?

BARON TURELURE (*in a low voice*): Sygne, save
your God and your King.

> (*He gazes at her fixedly.*

SYGNE (*returning his gaze*): No, no, you wicked
cripple, I am not for you!

BARON TURELURE: I swear to you I came here
knowing what I was doing.

SYGNE: Then do what you have to do as quickly
as possible.

BARON TURELURE: You would be wrong to doubt
me. You know I keep my word.

SYGNE: Then no longer doubt mine.

BARON TURELURE: Sygne de Coûfontaine, you who
play at being proud,
I shall buy you, and you will be mine.

SYGNE: Can you not take my property gratis?

BARON TURELURE: I shall take the land, and the
woman, and the name.

SYGNE: You will take me, Toussaint Turelure?

BARON TURELURE: I shall take the body and the
soul with it.
Your fathers shall be my fathers, and your children shall be my children.

SYGNE: Love will have worked this wonder.

BARON TURELURE: Justice at least, for see what
a price I am willing to pay for you.

SYGNE: I know. It is to you I owe my inheritance.

BARON TURELURE: To my mother who nursed you.

SYGNE: To your people who killed all mine.

BARON TURELURE: It is we then who have made you and reared you in two senses.

SYGNE: Monsieur le Préfet, you have my answer. It is enough.

Is there anything else that detains you here?

BARON TURELURE: One other small matter.

SYGNE: What?

BARON TURELURE: You have here the reports of the Councils.

Now you know that our new Theodosius is holding one this very moment in his capital.

Préameneu has asked me for a memorandum on this matter.

You will understand that I haven't Manzi's book at the Prefecture.

SYGNE: Take what you want.

BARON TURELURE: Here it is. I recognise the superb array of the folios in pig skin.

I like these beautiful Italian bindings.

> (*He limps across to that part of the library where the secret door is concealed.* SYGNE *quietly opens the drawer of the secretary and reaches into it with her hand.*

BARON TURELURE (*his back turned to* SYGNE): Here is the complete work. It's in perfect condition and without a spot of dust.

SYGNE: I will have it taken to your carriage.

BARON TURELURE: And what would happen, I wonder, if I were to carry a few volumes myself?

SYGNE: The weight of the Councils is too great for a lame prefect.

BARON TURELURE (*turning round quickly and looking* SYGNE *in the face*): What would happen? A lead bullet in my head, Aimed by that pretty hand yonder. You have some jewels in this little desk.

SYGNE: They are not without value to me.

BARON TURELURE: What is the good of making a big stain on the floor? And what would you do with my big wretched corpse? Would you put it also in this drawer with your other little secrets? I know this blessed house better than you, and you may well believe that I have set a cat to watch at every hole.

SYGNE: Toussaint Turelure, remember that I am armed and do not lead me into temptation.

BARON TURELURE: I will go then and leave you to your reflexions. Sygne de Coûfontaine, I leave you these two hours in which to decide.

(FATHER BADILON *enters.*

Father Badilon, I am your humble servant.

(*He goes out.*

Act Two: Scene Two

MONSIEUR BADILON (*a stout man evidently from the country*): That man at your house! What does this visit mean?

SYGNE: You know that the Prefect honours me with his sympathy.

MONSIEUR BADILON: But this visit at this time!

SYGNE: Baron Turelure
Came to ask for my hand.

MONSIEUR BADILON: He dared?

SYGNE: What audacity do you see in it? Baron, prefect, general, commander of I know not what, owner of all the vineyards of Mareuil, three or four châteaux (all encumbered with mortgages, it is true),
Is it not a reasonable match?
And as for his addressing me directly, what else could he do? Is it his fault that I have neither father nor mother? And I am old enough and sensible enough to manage alone in matters of this kind, as I do in others.

MONSIEUR BADILON: God delights not in bitter words.

SYGNE: I heard the sweet words in which he
revealed his heart to me.

MONSIEUR BADILON: And why did he choose just
this moment?

SYGNE: The sequel will make it plain to you.

MONSIEUR BADILON: Does he know perchance
that George is here?

SYGNE: He does.

MONSIEUR BADILON: Does he also know
Who this traveller is whom you received last night
beneath your roof?

SYGNE: Is it true then? You also tell me the same
thing . . .
The Pope. . . .

MONSIEUR BADILON: . . . Ravished from his prison
by your brother's hand . . .

SYGNE: O poor reckless George!

MONSIEUR BADILON: . . . Is here in hiding, and
entrusted to your keeping.

SYGNE (*turning towards the crucifix*): Woe be to
me, because Thou hast visited me!

MONSIEUR BADILON: But I hear Him answering:
Thou Thyself hast brought Me here.

SYGNE: I have held Thee in my arms and I know
Thou art heavy!

MONSIEUR BADILON: The burden is to the strong.

SYGNE: I understand now Thy aid and wherefore
I restored this house, not for myself.

MONSIEUR BADILON: But in order that the Father of all men might here find a shelter.

SYGNE: A precarious shelter and for a single night!

MONSIEUR BADILON: Can you devise no means of escape for the old man?

SYGNE: Toussaint guards every exit.

MONSIEUR BADILON: Is there no way of saving the Pope?

SYGNE: Turelure has entrusted his safety to my hand.

MONSIEUR BADILON: What does he ask in exchange?

SYGNE: The hand itself.

MONSIEUR BADILON: Sygne, save the Holy Father!

SYGNE: But not at this price! I say no!
I will not!
Let God take care of this man, who is His own,— my duty is towards my own!

MONSIEUR BADILON: You will betray then your fugitive father.

SYGNE: I will not betray my body and their body! I will not betray my name and their name!

MONSIEUR BADILON: You will betray your God instead.

SYGNE (*to the crucifix*): Bitterly hast Thou mocked me!

MONSIEUR BADILON: What have you asked of Him which He has not granted you?

What have you sought which is not yours?
The fruit of your labours you possess.

SYGNE: I possess!

MONSIEUR BADILON: Your race is safe in George whom you save
Preserving him for his children.

SYGNE: O God! It is in this that Thy hand appears!

MONSIEUR BADILON: I do not understand you.

SYGNE: His wife, you say, his children. . . .

MONSIEUR BADILON: Well?

SYGNE: All are dead.

MONSIEUR BADILON: Peace be with them! You then are free.

SYGNE: George remains.

MONSIEUR BADILON: What is there to preserve for him that is worth more than life?

SYGNE: Honour.

MONSIEUR BADILON: The honour with which thou shalt honour thy father and mother.

SYGNE: He is poor and lonely.

MONSIEUR BADILON (*to the crucifix*): There is another poorer and more lonely.

SYGNE: Know then, since I must tell you all, father,
What we did this very morning, he the last man and I the last woman of our race.

MONSIEUR BADILON: I am listening.

SYGNE: This morning we pledged our faith the one
to the other.

MONSIEUR BADILON: You are not yet married.

SYGNE: Married! Ah, this is more than any
marriage!
He gave me his right hand, as liege to vassal,
And I took an oath of fealty in my heart.

MONSIEUR BADILON: An oath in the night. Promises only, and neither deed nor sacrament.

SYGNE: Shall I take back my word?

MONSIEUR BADILON: High above the human word
is the Word which speaks in Pius.

SYGNE: I will not marry Toussaint Turelure!

MONSIEUR BADILON: George's life, too, is in his
power.

SYGNE: Let him die, as I am ready to die! Are
we eternal?
God gave me my life and I am ready to give it
back.
But my name is my own! My woman's honour
is mine alone!

MONSIEUR BADILON: It is good to possess something of one's own, in order to give it up.

SYGNE: George
Would perish, and this old man must remain
alive!

MONSIEUR BADILON: It is George who went to seek
him, and who brought him here.

SYGNE: This passing traveller, this old man who has nothing to give up save his breath!

MONSIEUR BADILON: Your guest, Sygne.

SYGNE: Let God do His duty for His part, as I do mine.

MONSIEUR BADILON: O my child, what is there more feeble and more helpless
Than God, since He can do nothing without us?

SYGNE: Miserable woman's weakness! Why did I not kill him without thinking
With that weapon I had in my hand? But I feared it might avail nothing.

MONSIEUR BADILON: Had you this criminal thought?

SYGNE: We should all have perished and I should not have had to make the choice!

MONSIEUR BADILON: It is very easy to destroy what has cost so much to save.

SYGNE: But to kill that man would be a good deed.

MONSIEUR BADILON: Of him, too, has God thought from all eternity, and he is His well beloved child.

SYGNE: Ah, I am deaf and hear not; I am a woman and not a nun, made of wax and manna like an *Agnus Dei!*
And if God loves my love for Him, and its nature, let Him in His turn understand my hatred,

which rises like my love, from the depth of my
heart and the treasure of my maidenhood!

Remember how since my birth I have lived face
to face with this man, ever watching him and
protecting myself from him, and making him
submit and serve me against his will!

And constantly through fear and detestation of
him there has sprung up a new strength in my
breast!

And now I must call him my husband, this beast!
must accept him and offer him my cheek!

But that I refuse! I say no! even if God incarnate should exact it of me.

MONSIEUR BADILON: That is why He does not
exact it.

SYGNE: What do you ask then in His name?

MONSIEUR BADILON: I ask nothing, and I exact
nothing, I only watch you, waiting,

Even as Moses watched the rock before him, when
he had smitten it.

SYGNE: What are you waiting for?

MONSIEUR BADILON: That for which it appears
you have been created and brought into the
world.

SYGNE: Must I save the Pope at the price of my
soul?

MONSIEUR BADILON: God forbid that we should
seek good through evil!

SYGNE: I will not give up my soul to the devil!

MONSIEUR BADILON: But already the spirit of violence possesses it,

Sygne, Sygne, and only last night you received in your mouth the body of Christ.

SYGNE (*in a hollow voice*): Have pity on me.

MONSIEUR BADILON (*with feeling*): O Thou great God! And you to whom I must speak words that affright me, have pity upon me!

It was your mother, the saintly countess Renée, who found me when I was only a poor little urchin, and made me priest for eternity.

And lo! Here am I asking from her daughter those things compared to which death is a small thing, I who am not worthy to touch your shoes!

I the stupid wretch, the gross man heavy with things of the flesh and with sins!

Here am I to whom God has given ministry over men and angels, even to these red hands has He given power to bind and to unbind!

All have perished, and it is I alone whom you now call your father, I the poor peasant!

But, at least, no father by blood could merit the name more than I, my beloved daughter, in the name of the Father and of the Son!

Pray to God that I may be a father to you, and not a sacrificial priest without bowels of compassion,

And that I may advise you in all calmness, in a
  spirit of moderation and of kindness.
For He does not ask of us that which is beyond
  our powers, but that which is well within them,
Delighting not in bloody sacrifice, but in the gifts
  His children make whole-heartedly.

SYGNE (*in a hollow voice*) :   Forgive me, for I have
  sinned.

> (*He opens his mantle and shows himself
> in a surplice, his violet stole crossing his
> breast.*

What! You have with you the Host?

MONSIEUR BADILON :   No. I have just taken it to
  Father Vincent in the wood.
This very morning as I left
(*in a low voice*) the Pope,
I was informed that the poor man had just had
  his legs crushed by an oak.
I came from his house. What a storm!
It called to mind the good old times of the Terror,
  when the sorcerer Quiriace used to pursue me
  relentlessly.
And when I used to spend the night in the hollow
  of a willow tree with our Lord upon my breast.

SYGNE (*kneeling*) :   Forgive me, father, for I have
  sinned.

MONSIEUR BADILON (*seated in an armchair beside
  her*) :   May He forgive you as I bless you.

106

SYGNE: I am guilty of violent words, of desire for death, of plans of murder.

MONSIEUR BADILON: Do you with all your heart renounce your hatred of every man and your desire to inflict injury?

SYGNE: I renounce them.

MONSIEUR BADILON: Proceed.

SYGNE (*in a low voice*): George
Of whom I spoke to you just now, father,
I love him.

MONSIEUR BADILON: But there is no wrong in that.

SYGNE: More than one ought to love any created thing.

MONSIEUR BADILON: Not so much, however, as God Himself Who made him.

SYGNE: Father, I have given him my heart!

MONSIEUR BADILON: It is not enough to love him apart from God.

SYGNE: But does God wish me to abandon and betray him?

MONSIEUR BADILON: Have patience with me, hear me, my well beloved child, for I am your shepherd who wishes you no ill.
It may happen that a woman must leave her wealth, her father and mother, her country and her betrothed
(And the thing is very hard, although the words are easy to say),

To withdraw into the desert at the foot of a cross,
to dress the wounds of the sick, to feed the poor,

To cherish and choose beyond all reason those who
seem as nothing to us;

She does it in the abundance of her devotion, and
her own salvation is not concerned therein.

So you, to save the Father of all men, according
to the call that has come to you,

May you renounce your love, your name, your
cause and your honour in this world,

Embracing your executioner and accepting him
as husband, even as Christ allowed Judas to par-
take of His body,

—Justice does not demand this.

SYGNE: Not doing it, I may remain sinless?

MONSIEUR BADILON: No priest will refuse you
absolution.

SYGNE: Is that true?

MONSIEUR BADILON: And I have more to say to
you: Give thought to this great sacrament of
marriage and take heed lest it be profaned.

That which God has created He consummates in
us. That which we sacrifice to Him He consecrates. He transforms the bread and the wine.

He consummates the oil. He makes the word
He has confided to us eternal. He makes a
sacrament like that of His own body

Of that confession by which the sinner condemns
himself to death.

Ah, how the heart of a priest shudders when such
a monster, who is the brother of Jesus, turning
towards him his distorted face, makes his confession through the orifice of his decaying body!

And even so He has sanctified in marriage the
consent which two beings seal one to another,
and one with another for eternity.

SYGNE: God does not desire, then, such a consent
from me?

MONSIEUR BADILON: He does not demand it, I
tell you with surety.

—And in the same way when the Son of God, for
men's salvation,

Tore Himself from His Father's bosom and
suffered humiliation and death

And that second death endured each day, which is
the mortal sin of those He loves,

No more did justice constrain Him.

SYGNE: Ah, I am not a God, but a woman!

MONSIEUR BADILON: I know it, poor child.

SYGNE: Is it for me to save God?

MONSIEUR BADILON: It is for you to save your
guest.

SYGNE: It was not I who invited him under my
roof.

MONSIEUR BADILON: It was your cousin who brought him.

SYGNE: I cannot! O my God, I cannot at this price!

MONSIEUR BADILON: It is well. You are acquitted of the blood of this just man.

SYGNE: I cannot go beyond my own strength.

MONSIEUR BADILON: My child, search the depths of your heart.

SYGNE: Behold it before you, laid open and tortured.

MONSIEUR BADILON: If your cousin's children were still alive, if it were a question of saving him and his,

Both the name, and the race, if he himself asked it of you—

This sacrifice which I propose to you—Sygne, would you make it?

SYGNE: Ah, who am I, a poor girl, to compare myself with the chief of my race? Yes, I would make it.

MONSIEUR BADILON: I hear it from your own mouth.

SYGNE: But he is my sire and my blood, my brother and my elder, the first and last of us all,

My master, my lord, to whom I have pledged my faith.

MONSIEUR BADILON: God was all that for you before ever your cousin was.

SYGNE: But He has no need of me! The Pope has His infallible promises!

MONSIEUR BADILON: But the world has them not, the world for which Christ did not pray.
Spare the universe this crime.

SYGNE: It is you who taught me, and did you not tell me how, each time when the Pope was well-nigh lost, God saved him?

MONSIEUR BADILON: Never without the help of some man and without his good will.

SYGNE: I live here all alone and know nothing of the world's affairs.

MONSIEUR BADILON: But you see at least that this is the hour of the Prince of this world, and Peter himself is in the hands of Napoleon.
What is to prevent him from making another Pope, like those emperors of the dark ages, or from stealing Him from Rome,
Like the ancient kings of France, in order to have Him with them?
That would be chaos! The heart itself out of place!
Oh, we are not alone here! Penitent soul, virgin, behold the immense host which surrounds us,
The blessed spirits in heaven, the sinners under our feet,

And the myriads of the human race, one upon another, awaiting your resolution!

SYGNE: Father, do not try me above my strength!

MONSIEUR BADILON: God is not above us, but
beneath.

And it is not according to your strength that I try
you, but according to your weakness.

SYGNE: So then I, Sygne, Countess of Coûfontaine,

Will marry of my own free will Toussaint Turelure, the son of my servant and of the wizard
Quiriace.

I will marry him before the face of the Triune
God, and I will swear fidelity to him, and he
shall place upon my finger the wedding ring.

He shall be flesh of my flesh and soul of my soul,
and that which Jesus Christ is for the Church,
Toussaint Turelure shall be for me, now and
forever.

He, the butcher of '93, reeking with the blood of
my people,

Shall take me in his arms each day, and there shall
be no part of me which is not his,

And of him shall I bear children in whom we
shall be united and blended.

All the wealth I have gathered together, not for
myself,

The property of my ancestors, and that of these
holy monks,

I will bring to him as my dowry; for him I shall
have suffered and laboured.

To the faith I have pledged I shall be false.
Betrayed by all, my cousin to whom I alone
remained loyal,—

I also, I last of all shall fail him!

This hand that he took in his on that Monday of
Pentecost,

In the sight of our parents,—his parents and mine,
exposed all together on that altar,—

I shall take back from him. Of these two hands
which just now were so passionately clasped,

Mine is false!

(Silence.

You are silent, father, and say nothing more to me!

MONSIEUR BADILON: I am silent, my child, and I
shudder!

I declare to you that neither I,

Nor the world, nor God Himself requires such a
sacrifice of you.

SYGNE: Who then constrains me?

MONSIEUR BADILON: Christian soul! Child of
God! It is for you alone to act of your own
will.

SYGNE: I cannot.

MONSIEUR BADILON: Prepare then. I will bless
and dismiss you.

SYGNE: My God! Yet Thou seest that I love Thee!

MONSIEUR BADILON: But not to the extent of suffering the spitting, the crown of thorns, the falling forward on the face, the stripping of garments and the cross.

SYGNE: Thou seest my heart!

MONSIEUR BADILON: But not through the great wound in my side.

SYGNE: Jesus! sweet friend!

Who has been my friend all this time save Thee? It is hard now to displease Thee.

MONSIEUR BADILON: But it is easy to do Thy will!

SYGNE: It is hard to separate myself from Thee for the first time.

MONSIEUR BADILON: But it is sweet to die in Me Who am the Truth and the Life.

SYGNE: Lord, if it be possible, let this cup pass from me!

MONSIEUR BADILON: Nevertheless Thy will be done and not mine!

SYGNE: At least, O my God, if I give up all to Thee,

Wilt Thou not also do one thing for me!

Delay not and take my wretched life with the rest!

MONSIEUR BADILON: Nevertheless to Thee alone is it given to know the day and the hour.

SYGNE (*in a hollow voice*): Lamb of God, which takest away the sins of the world, have mercy on me!

MONSIEUR BADILON: Even now He is with you.

SYGNE: Lord, not my will but Thine be done!

MONSIEUR BADILON: My child, is it consummated, then, the sacrifice?

SYGNE: . . . Not my will.

(*Silence.*

Lord, not my will but Thine be done! Lord, not my will but Thine be done!

MONSIEUR BADILON: My daughter, my well beloved child, do you see now how easy a thing God asks of you?

Is it overthrown at last, the temple of your pride? She is cast down, the Sygne whom God made not! Torn up by the very roots

Is that clinging love of self! And the created with her Creator has entered into the Eden of the cross!

"O my child, verily the joy is great that I reserve for my saints, but what sayest thou of my cup?" It is easy to die,

Easy to accept death and shame and to be buffeted upon the face, misjudged and scorned of all men.

All is easy except to grieve Thee. All is easy, O God, to the one who loves Thee

Except to do other than Thy blessed will.

(He rises.

And I, Thy priest, arise in my turn, and stand over
this sacrificed victim,

And I pray to Thee for her, as we pray over the
Elements at the mass.

Holy Father, Thou seest this lamb, who has done
what she could.

Take compassion on her now, and lay not upon
her an unbearable burden.

Have mercy, too, on me, priest and sinner, who
with my own hands have just sacrificed to Thee
my only child.

And you, my daughter, say that you forgive me
before I forgive you.

*(She makes a sign with her hand, and he
places his hand upon her head.*

My child, compose yourself and I will bless you,
and may the grace of God be with you!

*(She sinks down, her face to the ground,
and remains prostrate, with arms out-
stretched in supplication. Slowly he
makes over her the sign of the cross,
while through the windows enter the
golden rays of the setting sun.*

Act Three: Scene One

The château of Pantin near Paris. A large draw-ing-room on the ground floor with four French windows looking out on a terrace. Furniture in the formal style of the time of the Empire, bronzes and massive mahogany. A large portrait on the wall representing the Emperor Napoleon in coronation robes. The whole room is in disorder, and is covered with mud. It is the headquarters of the army defending Paris against the Allies, commanded by GENERAL BARON TOUSSAINT TURELURE, *Prefect of Seine, in his person uniting both civil and military powers.*

The sound of cannon in the distance. Then, quite near, the merry chime of three bells ringing for a baptism.

TOUSSAINT TURELURE *is standing,* SYGNE *is buried in a large armchair provided with a head rest.*[1]

TOUSSAINT TURELURE: You have my instructions. I must leave you now; excuse me. There's the procession leaving the church.

All my officers have gathered in the adjoining

---

[1] During the whole act Sygne shakes her head slowly from right to left in a nervous way, like a person saying No.

room and with hot cakes and a few bottles of Marne wine we are about to celebrate the entrance of little Turelure into the bosom of the Church.

Let us make the most of this leisure which your friends the Allies are allowing us.

We shall be sorry not to have the pleasure of your company, Madame. But business first!

A sad time it is when the father and mother cannot be present together at the baptism of their child!

SYGNE: You do not seem sad. You bear up well under this sad time.

TOUSSAINT TURELURE: True, 'pon my word! I have never been so happy!

War, business, a little intrigue, food for body and mind,

What more does a man need?

I was forgetting an affectionate wife and little Turelure who is about to have his first grain of salt put on the end of his tongue.

SYGNE: Why do you not manage your business yourself?

TOUSSAINT TURELURE: Mine is yours, there is no difference. I have seen you at work and I have great confidence in you.

And you see that I myself have my hands full.

Is it not fitting that after having restored the Pope
    to the Church, today
You should restore the King to his throne?
Moreover, it is not merely a matter of the country,
But of our joint wealth, which I want to consoli-
    date for this little son.

SYGNE: Which means
That I must complete the spoliation of my family?

TOUSSAINT TURELURE: For the benefit of your
    child who is the last male.
As for our gallant cousin, the generous Agénor,
    doubtless the King has compensation in store
    for him.

SYGNE: It will be for me to decide what to do.

TOUSSAINT TURELURE: I have full confidence in
    you.

SYGNE: Who is the King's plenipotentiary?

TOUSSAINT TURELURE: He is here. I am going to
    bring him to you.

SYGNE: I am ready.

TOUSSAINT TURELURE: No doubt you will come
    to an understanding.—I beg your pardon?

SYGNE: I said nothing.

TOUSSAINT TURELURE: It's that motion you make
    with your head.

        (*He puts his hand on the papers which are
        spread out on the table.*

Here are my conditions in which the dot of an *i* cannot be altered.

This is no time for discussion. France, for the moment, is myself, Toussaint Turelure,

Prefect of Seine, commander-in-chief of the Paris army,

To whom all civil and military powers have been entrusted by His Imperial and Royal Majesty.

SYGNE: You justify his confidence.

TOUSSAINT TURELURE: I am the man of France and not of any one master.

The Corsican has had his chance and I take mine where I find it.

SYGNE: Look out that he does not return with his big boots.

TOUSSAINT TURELURE: That is why we must choose our time cleverly, and it is not without a purpose that the Supreme Artist

          (*He makes a masonic sign.*

Has made me lame like a pair of scales.

All depends on Paris and Paris for a few moments is in my competent hands.

SYGNE: Do you think that all alone you can hold out here against three armies?

TOUSSAINT TURELURE: The Emperor has just won a victory at Saint-Dizier. I received the news of it a moment ago.

He directs me to hold out and put on a bold front,
whilst he fastens the three asses by the tail.

The road to Germany is barred, Alsace and the
Vosges are full of partisans, the Rhine fortresses
are not taken.

There are fine days ahead yet for the man of
Austerlitz.

And do not think that all these robbers are agreed;
there are ways of negotiating. You know I am
surrounded by *émigrés* and renegades.

SYGNE: You have no troops.

TOUSSAINT TURELURE: I have a lair. Let them
come and try to smoke me out of Paris.

I shall hold on tighter than a badger, I am impreg-
nable.

And you say I have no troops? Let the Emperor
of Russia come with his ragged bears and the
King of Prussia with his turnip-wood Johanne
Müllers!

I fear nothing so long as I have with me these
nurslings of Bellona, the firemen of Pantin, and
the National Guards of Saint-Denis, and the
volunteers of Popincourt!

Did you hear the cannon this morning?

SYGNE: Yes.

TOUSSAINT TURELURE: We walked into them, as
my orderly put it. Miloradovitch has been
wiped as clean as a bread plate.

Four hundred Wurtemburgers in pink trousers
   are lying in the vineyards of Noisy-le-Sec,
Their butter firkins on their heads, and their little
   fingers on the seam of their trousers,
The look of death still in their eyes and their little
   round noses turned to the left towards the Herr
   Adjutant "Habt Acht!"
—In honour of which we are about to drink this
   Mareuil wine.

SYGNE: All this is not serious.

TOUSSAINT TURELURE: I don't know.   But there
   is still another point which I implore you to
   consider.
If the Emperor falls there is but one single king
   possible for France.
There is Marie Louise's son, there is Oscar's
   papa.
Everything depends on me and on the hands into
   which I shall give the keys of Paris.
Whoever receives Paris,—all doubts will be at an
   end,—he is the incontestable heir.
I am a Frenchman!   To capitulate is repugnant
   to me,
Except to the son of Saint Louis
Whose most humble subject I wish to be,
Supporting on his very throne the foundations of
   our line.

SYGNE: The Turelure line.

TOUSSAINT TURELURE: A little gold circle above the T and in ten years it will sound like Tancrède or Tigranocerte.

And besides our cousin has no children, and the name which dies with him, the monarch can transfer.

SYGNE: I understand all.

TOUSSAINT TURELURE: I am sure of it. The fate of France I put back in your work basket.

(He puts in the papers.

There is nothing more for me to do except to introduce the other plenipotentiary to you.

SYGNE: Who is he?

TOUSSAINT TURELURE: It's a surprise. You'll see. The King is a man of sense.

We shall arrange everything in private.

(He goes out. The sound of the violins in the baptismal procession draws nearer.

TOUSSAINT TURELURE (*He comes in leading with him* VISCOUNT COÛFONTAINE): Sygne,

I present to you the Lieutenant and Plenipotentiary of His Majesty,

Our cousin George himself, whom politics has too long separated from us.

SYGNE: George!

GEORGE: Madame.

(He takes her hand and kisses it.

TOUSSAINT TURELURE: It is good to see them. I
swear, something is the matter with my eyes.
George, my wife has full power to negotiate
with you.

Adieu, George!

GEORGE: Adieu,—Toussaint!

(*Music. Deafening noise. Acclamations.
Tumult from the thronged house. Volley of musketry outside.*

TOUSSAINT TURELURE: *Tonnerre de Dieu,* they'll
murder one another! I gave orders that cartridges should not be given out!

(*He goes out.*

Act Three: Scene Two

SYGNE *hands over to* COÛFONTAINE *one of the papers left in her basket by the baron.* COÛFONTAINE *takes it and draws his spectacles out of his pocket. While he is reading she remains in her armchair, her eyes closed.*

Violent uproar in the adjoining room, the slamming of doors, bursts of laughter and loud talk, jingling of weapons and glasses, then the two violins sounding quite near and suddenly ceasing.

Crying of a new-born child.

GEORGE: Is it your child that is being baptised, Sygne? I saw the procession as I arrived.

SYGNE: Yes.

GEORGE: Why are you not at the festival?

SYGNE: My place is here.

> (*He resumes his reading, then stops again and listens. Somebody raps on a table and silence ensues.*)

VOICE OF TOUSSAINT TURELURE: Gentlemen, I present to you my son, Louis Agénor Napoleon Turelure!

> (*Applause.*

VOICE OF TURELURE: You have just been baptised a Christian with water by the priest,

And I baptise you a Frenchman, my little kitten, with this drop of the dew of Champagne on your tiny mouth.

Taste the wine of France, citizen!

> (*Laughter and applause.*

Let the Russian gentlemen wait! Let Field Marshal Benningsen and the Prince of Witzingerode do us the favour of being patient a moment!

Que diable! we can't attend to them all the time! We shall be at their service in a second.

For the moment let us enjoy the armistice which we have just arranged and drink in the best of wines to the health of this new-born babe.

> (*Loud noise of glasses. They drink. Cries of: Long live* TURELURE! *Long live Louis Agénor! Long live the Emperor!*

VOICE OF TURELURE: Pass the cake.

GEORGE: It was a good idea to preserve my name in this new shoot. The tremendous eloquence of Turelure moves me.

> (*Sound of trumpets in the distance.*

VOICE OF TOUSSAINT TURELURE: That is the Russian cavalry taking up its position. As for us let our trumpet be the cries of this child whom we have just baptised under the cannon!

Do you hear, Alexis Cowardovitch? It is the cry
of a free man! We don't care a hang for you,
Cossack!

(*Trumpets again.*

Are all these simpletons from the North going
to conquer France? They haven't spirit enough
for that.

There is still wine at Epernay! There will
always be enough of France to plague Europe,
to prick it behind and prevent it from eating
its grass peacefully, the old cow!

Gentlemen, I bring you good news: the Emperor
Napoleon has just won a great victory at Saint-
Dizier.

(*Cries: Long live the Emperor!*

And what of us? It seems to me we are holding
this place well enough.

We have Paris behind us and our enemies have
the Emperor and his eagles behind them!

Your health, gentlemen! *Sacrebleu!* everything
has not been taken from us so long as we have
this large corner of France, this little bit of
Turelure, and some cake!

(*Laughter. Applause. Acclamation.*

GEORGE (*resuming his reading*): An excellent
peroration and worthy of the exordium.

(*He finishes his reading and remains deep
in thought. Then he reads again, takes*

off his glasses, replaces them in his pocket, folds up the paper and puts it on the table. SYGNE *has not moved in her chair.*

GEORGE (*tapping the table lightly*): Sygne.

SYGNE (*straightening herself*): Yes?

GEORGE: It is with you I am to discuss this paper?

SYGNE: It is with me. The baron has given me full powers.

He has absolute confidence in me.

GEORGE: "He has absolute confidence in you." He is justified.

SYGNE: But there is nothing to discuss. There is no time.

GEORGE: Must I sign these conditions *hic et nunc?*

SYGNE: Not one iota can be changed.

GEORGE: And if I agree?

SYGNE (*showing a sealed letter*): Here is Turelure's surrender and the capitulation of Paris

To hand to His Most Christian Majesty.

GEORGE: Sygne, deliver up this paper to me.

SYGNE: I cannot.

GEORGE: Sygne, deliver up this paper, and I release you from the other.

SYGNE: I have promised.

GEORGE: You are certainly faithful to your promises.

SYGNE: At least I will be faithful to my shame.

GEORGE: May I not read the terms of surrender?

SYGNE: You must believe my word.

GEORGE: I believe you, Sygne.

SYGNE: George, what he says is true. He has shown me all and I have seen all. He has explained everything to me. I have gone over his reasons one by one, and I find no flaw in them.

The man is master of Paris, and he who receives Paris from his hand will be king.

GEORGE: It is then from Toussaint Turelure that the King of France is to expect his crown?

SYGNE: From him and from no other.

GEORGE: "The King swears to observe the Constitution.

The Budget will be voted each year by the people's representatives."

Thus does Toussaint capitulate, but the King will be compelled to abdicate.

SYGNE: I may not discuss the matter.

GEORGE: And the King by divine right becomes the King by Turelure's right.

SYGNE: And that, George,

Is what I propose and what you are going to accept.

GEORGE: I will not accept it.

SYGNE: Your orders are explicit.

GEORGE: What do you know of my orders?

SYGNE: If they were not what I think they are, you would not be here.

GEORGE: But what matters Parliament to your baron?

SYGNE: The possible alone matters to him.

GEORGE: This servant of the Tyrant—is it he who shall restrict the King?

SYGNE: All that one man alone can do the Emperor has proved to the world for all time.

GEORGE: Farewell then, O King whom I served, the image of God!

The King who, like unto God, recognised no limitation but his own essence.

Every man from the day of his birth used to accept the monarch as above him, eternally in his position by himself,

That he might learn at once that no man exists for himself alone, but for another, and that he might have this leader from birth.

And now, O King, at this latter end of my life,

With this hand which has fought for thee, I am about to sign thy downfall.

SYGNE: Rejoice because your eyes shall see what your heart desired.

GEORGE: There is something sadder to lose than life—the reason for living;

Sadder than to lose one's possessions is to lose one's hope,

More bitter than to be deceived is it to lose one's
   ideal.

SYGNE: But behold the King on his throne.

GEORGE: Do you call him the King? For my part
   I see nought but a Turelure crowned.

A chief Prefect administering the State for the
   general convenience, under oath, bound by a
   constitution,

To be dismissed as soon as one tires of him.

SYGNE: But for us at least, he exists;

He is the King still, by the great sacrifice we shall
   make for him;

If the lord perish let it not be before his vassal.

GEORGE: You speak of what Turelure asks of me?

SYGNE: Yes.

GEORGE: The general relinquishment and convey-
   ance to Turelure of all my rights, titles and
   possessions,

And the settlement after my death of all my rights
   on this heir you have given me.

All is granted without reservation.

SYGNE: O George, I wanted to cry out and contend
   at first.

GEORGE: You did not do so?

SYGNE: Have no fear.

GEORGE: I give you thanks, Sygne. I recognise
   you in that at least.

SYGNE: Come, give him all.

GEORGE: I suppose that is the part of the deed for which my brother-in-law cares most?

SYGNE: O George, give him everything!

GEORGE: What have I to give? You have everything already.

SYGNE: But the rights and the name are still yours.

GEORGE: Must I give them too?

SYGNE: Give them too.

GEORGE: But the name is not mine, the rights are not mine, the land is not mine, the alliance between the land and myself is not mine.

SYGNE: All is changed, George. There are rights no longer, there is nothing save possession. There is no longer an eternal alliance between earth and man save in the grave alone.

And the hands which were clasped have been separated.

And yours is no longer good for anything but to write and resign.

GEORGE: Let him keep all, I will ask nothing back from him.

SYGNE: But you must write your consent.

GEORGE: I shall not capitulate.

SYGNE: Are you then your sovereign's enemy?

GEORGE: I cannot yield my honour.

SYGNE: What else have you to yield?

GEORGE: Let there be one man at least in the world who betrays not!

SYGNE: Yield, betray, renounce. O George, give him that also! Dear brother, do not prevent us from attaining the end!

GEORGE: We shall not attain the end, in this child.

SYGNE: All is at an end for me with you.

GEORGE: The rest is cut off, true. All our names and all our wealth
Accumulate on this child's head.

SYGNE: Do you accuse me of a vile thought?

GEORGE: The shame you have purchased is enough.

SYGNE: Purchased by the travail of my soul and the sweat of my brow!

GEORGE: It is your own.

SYGNE: It is my own indeed!
It is my possession which shall not be taken from me, this shame that is more lasting than praise!
It will go with me to the grave and beyond, it is graven on me like a stone, it is a part
Of these bones which will be judged!

GEORGE: Sister, why did you do it?

SYGNE (*crying out*): George!
It was the bad blood in me which spoke, and I thought myself so strong and reasonable!
Remember that ancestor of ours who fought with the Burgundian against Joan, and the one who became a renegade,
And that Nogaret also, from whom we are descended, who struck the Pope in the face.

Great and unheard of things, our heart is such
that it cannot withstand them.
And lo, now I stand alone in an enemy's land,
Like that Agénor of olden times whose château
stood on the other side of the Dead Sea, on the
slope of Arnon.

GEORGE: And so our hands also have been un-
clasped, and the honour of our coat of arms is
besmirched.
And this hand was torn from me last of all, this
hand which I held in mine on the morning of
that sacrifice which was offered up!

SYGNE: I have torn away my hand, and do not you
tear away my heart!

GEORGE: All that binds one man to another,
All this by your hand was still assured me: child,
sister, father and mother, protegée, comforter,
Wife, vassal, companion in arms. All this still
existed for me while I clasped your hand in
mine, and knew the strength of fellowship.
What oath is there you have not broken? What
fealty is there you have not withdrawn from
me?

SYGNE: That oath at least is unbroken which I took
at my baptism.

GEORGE: You ought not then to have taken any
other.

SYGNE: But by what can we swear if not by God?

GEORGE: God has many friends whilst I had but
a single lamb.

SYGNE: I saved the Father of men.

GEORGE: And you ruined your brother.

SYGNE: Be my judge then, I am willing.

GEORGE: God is your judge, and I am the appellant
at His tribunal, and the law He has made Himself cannot alter.
And I shall summon you to produce my glove,
for that which is once given
Cannot be taken back either on earth or in heaven.

SYGNE: I fear nothing of God, and the Lord cannot further abase me,
For that which is cast on the ground cannot fall
lower,
And I do not ask a higher place.

GEORGE: You have been faithless to your promise.

SYGNE: A great prize was offered me.

GEORGE: You have been faithless in love.

SYGNE: Have I grieved you much, George?

GEORGE: Too much. It was unnecessary and my
cup was full.
Now I am about to die and suffer damnation, and
I have eternity before me void of all consolation.
Could not this short hour be given me?
Could not one single faithful heart be left to me?
one single Veronica in whom to hide my face

so that none might behold it in that hour when the heart succumbs?

SYGNE: It was I alone, it was I alone who did this, who did this of my own accord. Do not speak one word against God!

On my wicked heart alone rests all the blame!

GEORGE: You have been faithless to me. My child has turned from me in bitterness.

SYGNE: May God take my place, wretched that I am, and discharge what I cannot pay!

GEORGE: It was not necessary to do it.

The faithlessness which deceives true love

God Himself cannot redeem.

He could not do it though He should create a new heaven and a new earth!

Do you enjoy your God, and I will shut you out of my heart.

Had I a paradise to expect after this life?

Or am I like those men of today who are satisfied with ideas and with words of no real meaning?

My lot was with living men. Society for me was the possession of a man's heart and not of any idea. With my companions was my lot, my faith and my hope, and my heart in a heart made like unto my own.

And you, in this last hour of my life, you abjure me solemnly, as a Jew who tears his raiment from top to bottom.

—Do not shake your head like that.

SYGNE: My humiliation is too great. Alas, there is no more grief for me, though my soul thirsts for it as thirsts the parched ground.

I am cut off from tears.

For me no more sorrow is possible, all fresh suffering heaped upon the old is as consolation.

GEORGE: And what is it I must do?

SYGNE: Come with me where there is no more sorrow.

GEORGE: And no more honour?

SYGNE: Neither name nor honour.

GEORGE: Mine is whole.

SYGNE: But what is the use of its being whole? The seed that is put in the ground

Of what use is it unless it decays?

GEORGE: The flesh decays, but the rock remains unchangeable.

SYGNE: Earth is the same for us both.

GEORGE: But I have not betrayed it. I have honoured this land which was my own possession,

In order that it might feed not only the flesh but also a heart

That was faithful, the earth itself being faithful.

SYGNE: I am going to feed it in my turn.

GEORGE: Perjured one! This land you have sold

is no longer yours, and your slave-name is no longer its feudal name.

SYGNE: I have loved it more than you.

GEORGE: Who could love it more than an exile?

SYGNE: You love only the surface.

GEORGE: It is my land and my possession, and is like no other.

SYGNE: And I possess the heart and the roots of it. All earth is the same at a depth of six feet.

GEORGE: Do you not look forward to a resurrection?

SYGNE: Do not speak of the things you understand not.

Yet even if there were none the happiness of dying is great enough in itself.

GEORGE: You say well. That at least is true.

SYGNE: O George, how foolish we both have been! It is pitiable! There we were absurdly engaged to be husband and wife, as though we still had a place among men.

Have men still need of us among them? No more than of Coucy and its towers.

And do you count so much on being a landlord, as others are shepherds or millers?

Men no longer have need of a higher one in their midst.

We were made to give and to receive, but not to share.

Come then with me, taking my hand,

Not like husband and wife who are rooted in each other,

But take my hand since you will see me no more. O brother, I have not changed! and my other hand is linked to the chain of my departed ones who are dead.

George, what have you to do in this life? Long enough have we been a burden to men.

Long enough have we harshly compelled them to live not for themselves but for us, as we ourselves lived for God and the King.

Now, every man is going to live for himself at his ease and there will no longer be God or master.

The earth is large, and every man may go his own way, for now are they free after the manner of animals.

But do we care to be free? there is no liberty for the nobleman.

Or equal?

Or brothers, for there will no longer be names or family, and you alone are my brother!

GEORGE: You are no longer my sister.

SYGNE: Yes, George, I am.

GEORGE: I will not take your false hand again.

SYGNE: It is true that I am a traitor! I have given up everything and myself too! all that was dead in me.

The King is dead: the Chief is dead. But I have
saved the eternal Priest.

God lives for us, so long as we still have His
word with us, and a little bread and His sacred
hand which binds and unbinds.

GEORGE: It has unbound yours.

SYGNE: Then I go alone and unbound towards the
subterranean sun.

GEORGE: But whilst we yet live let us finish what
we have to do.

SYGNE: Will you sign these papers?

GEORGE: I will sign them all, in the King my
master's name and my own.

(He takes them, reads and signs them.
Should I not expect some trickery of your husband?

SYGNE: His orders are already written, he has
shown them to me. The couriers are waiting.
His self-interest protects you.

In one hour Paris will be disarmed, and Mont-
martre in the hands of your friend.

GEORGE: Here is my will, here is the new alliance.
But have I not read that there is no testament
without death and no alliance without the shed-
ding of blood?

SYGNE: May it be mine!

GEORGE: Do not tempt me.

SYGNE: If you have no God be a man at least, and
if there is no justice create it for yourself, and
act in accordance with your own law.
Whoever has been faithless to human promise, let
him die! I am ready.

GEORGE: No, no! I will not kill my poor child!

SYGNE: O George, you love me still!

GEORGE: But at any rate I will free you from that
man.

SYGNE: Do not kill him.

GEORGE: Do you treasure his life so much?

SYGNE: As little as my own.

GEORGE: He shall die then by my hand.

SYGNE: Why concern yourself with that man?

GEORGE: I shall free the King from his promises.

SYGNE: He who is dead
Can no longer give back his promise.

GEORGE: Writing is not speech and can be destroyed.

SYGNE: Shall I then appeal to you in vain?

GEORGE: In vain.

SYGNE: Do what you will.

GEORGE: At your service.

> (*He retires, walking slowly as far as the
> French window, and disappears.*

Act Three: Scene Three

                    (TOUSSAINT TURELURE *enters.*
TURELURE: Well, Madame?
            (*She hands him the papers in silence. He
            takes them, verifies them at a glance, and
            immediately rings a bell.*
It is for me to do what remains to be done.
                            (*A servant enters.*
Send in the couriers whom I ordered to be in
    readiness.
                        (*Several officers enter.*
These orders to my generals. The whole army
    must retire to Paris. The National Guard is
    disbanded, the reserves are to go to Versailles,
Under command of the Duke of Raguse.
By order of the Emperor. Lose no time.
            (*He distributes sealed letters. The couriers
            leave.*
To Sygne:
I recalled our cousin's excellent trick.
                            (*He rings.*
Monsieur Lafleur.
                    (*Monsieur Lafleur enters.*
Monsieur Lafleur, take these papers to the per-
    son—you know to whom—

                        142

And say that I lay myself at his feet.

> (*Monsieur Lafleur goes out.*
> (*He rings. Two other couriers enter.*

These papers to Dalberg and Talleyrand.

And say that the appointment is here this very night.

> (*They go out.*
> (*He rings. An officer enters.*

TURELURE (*straightening himself*): When three o'clock strikes, order the flag to be lowered.

> (*The officer goes out.*

That's a good deal of work done in a short time.

> (*He remains standing and throwing out his chest as if "at attention," with head erect, his arms rigid beside his body, his hands bent backwards. The clock makes a prolonged grinding noise and is about to strike.*

TURELURE: The hour strikes.

> (*At this moment* COÛFONTAINE *appears at the window. The first stroke of the hour is heard.* TURELURE *immediately arms himself. Two shots ring out at the same time.* SYGNE *throws herself at a bound in front of him. The second stroke is heard. The room is filled with smoke. When it clears* SYGNE *is seen stretched out on the floor in a pool of*

blood. The third stroke is heard. TURE-
LURE *quickly strides over the body and
hastens to the window. He is seen
behind the broken panes leaning towards
the ground, then moving off, as if drag-
ging behind him a burden that is not
seen.*

Pause.

TURELURE *re-enters. Several servants have
gathered in the room.*

TURELURE (*in a voice of command*) : The baroness
is wounded. A deplorable accident has oc-
curred. Let a bed be made for her on that
table. Send for the doctor and Father Badilon!
As for me, I am busy with State affairs.

(*He goes out.*
(*The curtain falls and remains down for
a few moments.*

Act Three: Scene Four

> (*The same room at sunset. It is nearly dark.* SYGNE *is lying on a large table in one corner of the room.* MONSIEUR BADILON *is by her side. A single candle is burning in a tall silver candlestick.*

MONSIEUR BADILON: Sygne, my child, do you hear me?

> (*Long pause. The eyelids flutter.*

MONSIEUR BADILON (*lower*): Do you hear me?

SYGNE: What does the doctor say?

MONSIEUR BADILON: My daughter, rejoice.

SYGNE: It is death, then, that he heralds?

MONSIEUR BADILON: Your time of trial is over.

> *She commences the familiar shaking of her head, but is soon overcome.*

MONSIEUR BADILON (*listening intently to her*): "No more joy . . ." What do you say? Don't move your head like that. You will open your wound again.

What do you say? "No more joy, . . . no more blood . . ." (*He repeats.*

"No more grief to suffer, no more joy to delight me."

(*Speaking to himself*) : She is exhausted.
But you are going to heaven while I remain in this desolation.

SYGNE: Is he . . .

MONSIEUR BADILON: Is he dead? Your cousin George?

(*The eyelids flutter.*

He is dead. The bullet went straight to his heart.

SYGNE: . . . the time . . .

MONSIEUR BADILON: Time to give him absolution? No. I was summoned too late. He was already dead.

(*Silence.*

I add this bitterness. But . . .

SYGNE: It does not make me uneasy.

MONSIEUR BADILON: True. God Almighty provides.

SYGNE: Together.

MONSIEUR BADILON: The two Coûfontaines together, in turn preceding one another.

SYGNE: The perjury.

MONSIEUR BADILON: It is now redeemed with your blood.

SYGNE: The oath.

MONSIEUR BADILON: Not broken in any way, but consummated. In God the Son,
Who is seated on the right hand, and in Whom is every promise made perfect.

SYGNE: With him.

MONSIEUR BADILON: With you for ever, O my master and my chief. *Coûfontaine, adsum.*

SYGNE: Jesus.

MONSIEUR BADILON: Our Lord Jesus is with you.

SYGNE: With him.

MONSIEUR BADILON: With you, the righteous and the sinner inseparable, and the work will not be separated from the workman, or the sacrifice from the altar, or the vestment from the blood in which it is soaked.

SYGNE: All.

MONSIEUR BADILON: All is finished, all is done as it was ordained, the bride having received absolution is laid in her nuptial garments.

I have finished my work, I have perfected my child for heaven.

And I remain alone.

The child of my soul takes wing, and I the old useless priest remain alone.

SYGNE (*a half turn of her head*).

MONSIEUR BADILON: Bride of the Lord!

I have absolved you, and do you absolve me in my turn,

Also this hand which I have laid on you as one who consecrates and who sacrifices!

And tell me you forgive me

That evil which I did you,

Those words I spoke to you, my poor dove, I a
  sinner,

By the command of God, my master, to the dismay
  of my heart,

In order that Peter should be saved and your
  crown made perfect.

SYGNE: . . . (*she moves her eyes*).

MONSIEUR BADILON: My hand? You want me to
  raise my hand again, and hold it in front of
  your eyes?

SYGNE: . . . (*she moves her lips*).

MONSIEUR BADILON: Thus the poor dying lamb
  takes in its harmless mouth the hand that has
  cut its throat!

It is not my hand that you kiss, O my daughter,
  but the Christ in His priest who anoints and
  pardons.

The hand of the consecrated priest who has so
  often given you communion and who every
  morning elevates

The Son of God in the sacraments,

And Whom you are about to see face to face.
                    (*He falls on his knees by the bed*.

And now at last I may be a coward and show you
  my heart!

No man has loved you as I have, with that love
  which the people of this world understand not,

For God Himself, Who spoke through my mouth
and Who heard through your ears,

Was He not also in both our hearts?

Glory to God who gave the sublime soul to be
guided by the soul the most lowly!

And when you knelt at my side in the tribunal of
penitence,

It was I who in the deep gloom was amazed and
prostrated myself before you.

Alas, I had only a single child and behold they
have slain her!

Remember your shepherd, little lamb, you who
so often came to take the celestial food from his
hands.

(Silence.

SYGNE (with a bitter smile which little by little becomes more marked) : . . . So saintly?

MONSIEUR BADILON : And what greater love is
there than this to lay down one's life for one's
enemies?

SYGNE (smiles).

MONSIEUR BADILON : Did you not throw yourself
in front of your husband to shield him?

SYGNE (almost indistinctly) : Too good . . .

MONSIEUR BADILON : Death? What do you say?

(He leans over her.

SYGNE (she moves her lips).

149

MONSIEUR BADILON: . . . "Too good a thing to leave for him."

And do you pretend to know your intentions better than God Himself?

> (*Silence. She begins to have difficulty in breathing.*

But I know that you have forgiven him already.

> (*Silence. She makes a sign in the negative.*

Sygne! at this moment when you are about to appear before God. Tell me you have forgiven him.

> (*Sign in the negative.*

Shall I have your little one brought up to you?

> (*Sign in the negative.*

What? Sygne, do you understand me? Your child? . . .

SYGNE (*in a distinct voice*): No.

> (*Silence. The agony begins.*

MONSIEUR BADILON (*rising*): Death is near. Christian soul, say with me the petition of recommendation and the prayers of hope and charity.

SYGNE (*sign in the negative*).

MONSIEUR BADILON: Sygne, soldier of God! Courage! Courage till the last!

SYGNE: All is finished.

MONSIEUR BADILON: *Coûfontaine, adsum!*

SYGNE: All is finished.

MONSIEUR BADILON: Jesus, Son of David, *adsum!*
        (*Silence. The death rattle begins.*
All is ended. The last drop has been drained.
        (*Silence.*
Lord, have mercy on this child whom Thou
  gavest me, and whom I give to Thee in turn.
Eli! I entreat thee in the awful secrecy of the last
  hour.
Lord, in Whom all the ages are as one instant
  which cannot be divided,
Have mercy on these two souls about to appear
  before Thee at the same moment, whom Thou
  madest brother and sister.
And accept the blood poured out, and this exchange between them made in the flash of the
  thunderbolt.
    (*Suddenly* SYGNE *raises herself and extends
    both her arms above her head in the sign
    of the cross; then, falling back on her
    pillow, she gives up the ghost, blood
    gushing from her mouth.*
    FATHER BADILON *piously wipes her mouth
    and face. Then bursting into tears, he
    falls on his knees at the foot of the bed.*

Act Three: Scene Five

Behind the glazed windows, and following TOUS-
SAINT TURELURE, *appears a man holding a stable
lantern, followed by four more carrying on a door
removed from its hinges the body of* COÛFONTAINE
covered by his cloak. They enter.

TOUSSAINT TURELURE: Priest, how is the baroness?

> *(No answer.*
Madame.
> *(He takes the lantern and holding it near
> the dead woman's face, he examines it.
> Then putting the light down on the
> floor, he makes the sign of the cross.
> To the people who are in the background:*
Come forward!
Let my cousin's body be brought and laid on this
table,—next to my wife's, I say!
So that the two Coûfontaines may lie side by side,
And that those who have been separated in life
may share the same bed in death.
And let the closed fist be placed in the open hand.
> *(They do as he bids.* COÛFONTAINE *is laid
> by the side of* SYGNE, *and the white flag*

with fleur-de-lis is spread over them. But
SYGNE'S *open hand slips from under the*
cloth and they cannot put it back. On
a table at the head of the funeral couch,
covered with a cloth, a crucifix is placed
between two lighted candles and a vessel
of holy water with the aspersorium.

Meanwhile the noise outside of an army
marching and endless troops passing has
gradually increased till it shakes the
earth. The noise of horses, the rumbling
of artillery and waggons.

Then all at once the sound of bells and of
a carriage drawn by horses urged on at
full speed which suddenly stop in front
of the house. Uproar. Doors are
opened violently and all the house is
filled with light. Suddenly the double
doors seem to be burst open from without
and a great cry is heard:

The King!

    (*Two lackeys enter bearing torches and*
behind them the KING OF FRANCE.

TOUSSAINT TURELURE (*advancing to meet him*):
Sire, welcome to your own kingdom!

        (*He kneels and kisses his hand.*

THE KING: Rise. I am pleased to recognise in
you the most useful of my subjects.

(He looks round him. His son, brother, and the officers of his suite have come in behind and surround him.

TURELURE: May your Majesty deign to excuse the disorder of this house.

THE KING: It resembles that of France. Poor old dwelling!

From cellar to attic nothing has been left in its place. Everything has suffered conscription.

But we bring peace with us.

(Flattering murmurs amongst his suite. The KING sees the death bed before which FATHER BADILON is still in prayer, and raising his eyebrow slightly towards TURELURE questioningly, he looks at him for the first time.

TURELURE: May your Majesty excuse my inability to hide from him the grief of my house.

THE KING: Who is it?

TURELURE: My wife,

Descended from the purest and most loyal blood of France.

THE KING (*recognising the arms*): *Coûfontaine, adsum.*

And who is the other corpse?

TURELURE: George Agénor, my cousin, your faithful servant and lieutenant.

Both fell at the same time.

A deplorable misunderstanding, the awful and
strange mistake of this sudden crisis.

> (*The* KING *majestically approaches the bed
> and sprinkles it with holy water. Then
> he hands the aspersorium to his son, who
> does the same, then his brother and the
> officers of his suite. And, last of all,*
> TURELURE, *who performs the rite with
> compunction.*

THE KING (*back in the middle of the room*): I
shall know how to recognise such services, and
the blood shed in my cause.

TURELURE: A noble name has died out.

THE KING: It has not died out. I know you have
a son.

> (*An usher enters and speaks a word in*
> TURELURE'S *ear.*

TURELURE: Sire, . . .

THE KING: Speak.

TURELURE: The Civil and Ecclesiastical Estates
Have arranged a meeting in this house to greet
your Majesty.

THE KING: Good. I will give them audience at
once.

TURELURE (*pointing to the left*): Here, on the left,
are the delegates of the legislative body, the
State Council, the Courts and the conservative
Senate.

THE KING: Open the door.
> (*The double doors are opened. Noise on
> the right.*

THE KING: On the right.

TURELURE: On the right are the bishops of France
who throw themselves at your Majesty's feet.
You know that the Usurper had called together a
Council here,
In order to formulate the liberties of the Gallic
Church, under the protection of the military
power.

THE KING: De Pradt and Talleyrand shall present
them to me.
Open the door.
> (*The door on the right is opened. An
> usher enters and speaks to* TURELURE.

TURELURE: Sire,
The delegation from the Marshals of France asks
to be presented to your Majesty.

THE KING: Let them enter!
> (*The delegation of Marshals enters.*

THE SENIOR MARSHAL: Sire, the Army
Is happy to render homage to its sovereign.
> (*He salutes.*
> (*The* KING *graciously grasps his hands as
> if the Marshal were about to kneel.*

Rise!

The King of France is proud to see your swords around his throne restored.

It is not to the foreigner that you have given them, but to the King of France, Louis your King, who alone

(Majestically.

Is peace.

(Slight pause.

Cherish glory! it is yours and will not be taken from you,

And if there is any shame to assume for the safety of the people,

Let the King alone assume it, as is befitting for the head of a family.

I return to put myself between my people and the enemy.

I return to you.

Not with, but through your enemies, at this hour when France is wounded, and my hands alone here are without weapons and may not hold any.

And it is true we suffer violence.

But consider fairly that Europe cannot do without France,

And this empire they fashioned for you was no longer France, it was no longer her size and shape,

Not extended, I should say, but diminished.

THE MARSHAL: We are your loyal soldiers and the most faithful of your subjects.

THE KING: Remain and be our witnesses.

> (*He advances to the centre of the room, and turning a little towards the right, then towards the left, says in a loud voice.*

And all you, Bishops, Officers, Civil and Ecclesiastical Estates, whose conduct I welcome,

Be witnesses of the act that I am about to perform.

> (*He returns towards the table that has been prepared, on which are placed candles, pens, parchment, wax and the Great Seal of France.*

> *Enter the* KING OF ENGLAND, *the* KING OF PRUSSIA, *the* EMPEROR OF AUSTRIA, *the* EMPEROR OF RUSSIA, *the* PAPAL NUNCIO.

My brothers, welcome to my kingdom,

And accept my thanks for your loyal service.

Sovereigns of Europe!

Be witnesses of this new covenant which the King of France will now sign with his people.

> (*He turns slowly towards the window where the glow of several fires appears.*

What are these fires?

TURELURE: It is nothing.   A few poor quarters of Paris burning, a good riddance!

Some stubborn fellows that Monsieur de Raguse has succeeded in bringing to reason.

The firebrand of the Revolution is dying out in stench and smoke.

THE KING (*with scorn*): Those extravagances have ended.

> (*He sits down heavily.*

And the King with France begins anew according to the legitimate order.

> (*He is sitting behind the table between the two candles. On his left,* TURELURE; *on his right the* DAUPHIN, *the* HIGH CHAN-CELLOR; *behind, the* SOVEREIGNS. *In front, grouped in the windows, the* MAR-SHALS. *On the right and left the* BISHOPS, *the* CIVIL *and* ECCLESIASTICAL ESTATES, *and* STATE OFFICIALS *in rows extending beyond the two open doors.*
>
> *The* KING *with his big, round eyes looks slowly around the assembly, then speaks to* TURELURE:

Count!

TURELURE (*chuckling*):   I'm a count!

THE KING: Kindly bring seats for their Majesties.

THE END

ACTING VERSION

Substituted for Scenes IV and V of the Original Text

DRAMATIS PERSONÆ

of *l'Otage*

As originally acted at the "Théatre de l'Œuvre"
on the 5th of June, 1914.

SYGNE DE COÛFONTAINE	MLLE. EVE FRANCIS
LE PAPE	MR. JOSÉ SAVOY
CURÉ BADILON	MR. LUGNÉ-POE
LE VICOMTE ULYSSE AGÉNOR GEORGES DE COÛFONTAINE ET DORMANT	MR. MAX BARBIER
LE BARON PUIS COMTE TOUSSAINT TURELURE	MR. JEAN FROMENT

Act Three, Scene Four: Acting Version

TURELURE: Good day, Sygne.

        (She makes an effort as if to speak, but cannot.
Do you hear me? Cannot you speak?
Try, though. I can read the words on your lips.

        (Her lips move, but no sound escapes.
Dead? Is George dead?

        (Sygne assents.
I regret to say he is.

        (Her lips move.
The priest? I tell you he is dead.
Too late. He is too late.
The bullet struck his forehead. He is dead—
But I am alive,
Thanks to you, dear Sygne.

        (Silence.
Without priest, without confession,
And in a state of mind, alas! which leaves us some
   doubts as to his salvation.

        (Silence.
What? I cannot hear you.
Infinite?
God's mercy is infinite? True, God's mercy is infinite.
His justice, too. *Nescio vos* has He written. I know
   you not.
It is the Father who speaks thus.

        (Silence.

It is useless for you to say no.

(Silence.

But I, Sygne, what gratitude I owe you!

(Silence.

You saved my life at the price of your own.

O mystery of conjugal love! O devotion worthy of
antiquity!

It was written of you, as of far-distant Ruth: "Thy
people shall be my people, and thy gods shall be
my gods. . . ."

What is a brother to you compared with the husband
you have chosen?

Ah, I hope that henceforth where I am you will be
with me, and that our bones may lie side by side in
the same grave.

(Silence.

You say no? But I say yes, and it is I who am the
stronger.

I know you better than you do yourself, and this last
deed reveals you at length.

Love is a stronger bond than blood. And who shall
know you better, my dear Sygne,

Than that husband to whom was revealed the secret
of your virgin body?

(Silence.

At least your sacrifice was not in vain.

The King returns to France.

(Silence.

The King is here again and I am his first minister.

(Silence.

Coûfontaine lives once more in our dear child. Will
you not see him and kiss him?

> (*Sign in the negative.*

What? You do not want to see your child?

> (*Sign in the negative.*

This is serious.

> (*Silence.*

Sygne, it is useless to hide it from you. I am afraid
that for you, too, the hour of death is near.

Father Badilon is not far away. Should I send for
him?

> (*Silence.*

Sygne, do I understand rightly? You do not say anything?

> (*Silence.*

You are holding out against me, Sygne. But you cannot hide from me the tears which flow from your
eyes.

> (*Silence. She is crying.*

Do you think that I do not understand you?

> (*Silence.*

You are unwilling to forgive me. You are unwilling
that the priest should compel you to forgive.

You were willing to give me your life, death was too
dear a thing to give to me.

But not to forgive me. And yet it is the necessary
condition of your salvation.

> (*Silence.*

> (TURELURE, *slowly, as if spelling with his lips.*

"I can do no more," do you say?

> (*Silence.*

165

(TURELURE, *as before.*

"All . . is . . finished . . to . . to . . the . . depths . .

"All . . is . . crushed . . out . . to . . the . . very . . last . .
  drop." No, it is not.

Duty remains.

Let me implore you in the name of your eternal salvation.

In truth, you offend me who believe in these things no
  more than your brother.

(Silence. Sign in the negative.

So great is the hate you bear me.

Then what was our marriage?

Marriage is a sacrament. It is not the priest who
  makes marriage, but consent alone.

And like bread at the eucharist, the "yes" is the material of that permanent communion.

How complete ought that to be which makes of two
  souls one soul in a single body?

A great sacrament, said the Apostle.

(Silence.

Sygne, what ought I to think of that "yes" you gave
  me?

(Silence.

Your intentions were good? Evasion.

It was a question of saving the Pope? No.

No end can justify an evil deed.

None. (Silence.

Sygne, do you hear me? Yes, I see that you still hear
  me. Ah! proud girl, you do not waver.

(Silence.

You have been unable to complete your sacrifice and
you recoil at the last moment.

Damnation, Sygne! eternal separation from the God
Who made you,

And Who made me, too, in His own image: yes,
although you refuse to forgive me.

From the God Who summons you to this supreme
moment, and Who calls upon you, the last of your
race!

Coûfontaine! Coûfontaine! Do you hear me?

What! you refuse! you betray!

Rise, though you are dead already! it is your Suzerain
who calls! What, are you a deserter?

Rise, Sygne! Rise, soldier of God! and give Him your
glove,

Like Roland on the field of battle when he restored his
glove to the archangel Saint Michael.

Rise and cry: *Adsum*, Sygne! Sygne!

   (*He appears enormous and mocking as he
   stands over her.*

Coûfontaine, adsum! Coûfontaine, adsum!

   (*She makes a violent effort, as if to rise, lifts
   her hand towards heaven and falls back
   again.*

     (TURELURE *in a lower tone as if afraid.*

Coûfontaine, adsum!

   (*Silence. He takes the torch and passes the
   light before her eyes, which remain motion-
   less and fixed.*